UNIVERSALLY PREFERABLE BEHAVIOUR

UNIVERSALLY PREFERABLE BEHAVIOUR

A RATIONAL PROOF OF SECULAR ETHICS

• • •

Stefan Molyneux

ISBN-13: 9781975653743
ISBN-10: 1975653742

Table of Contents

FOREWORD

• • •

IN MANY FAIRY TALES, THERE lives a terrible beast of stupendous power, a dragon or a basilisk, which tyrannizes the surrounding lands. The local villagers tremble before this monster; they sacrifice their animals, pay money and blood in the hopes of appeasing its murderous impulses.

Most people cower under the shadow of this beast, calling their fear "prudence," but a few – drunk perhaps on courage or foolhardiness – decide to fight. Year after year, decade after decade, wave after wave of hopeful champions try to match their strength, virtue and cunning against this terrible tyrant.

Try – and fail.

The beast is always immortal, so the villagers cannot hope for time to rid them of their despot. The beast is never rational, and has no desire to trade, and so no negotiations are possible.

The desperate villagers' only hope is for a man to appear who can defeat the beast.

Inevitably, a man steps forward who strikes everyone as utterly incongruous. He is a stable boy, a shoemaker's son, a baker's apprentice – or sometimes, just a vagabond.

This book is the story of my personal assault on just such a beast.

This "beast" is the belief that it is impossible to define an objective, rational, secular and scientific ethical system. This "beast" is the illusion that morality must forever be lost in the irrational swamps of gods and governments, enforced for merely pragmatic reasons, but forever lacking logical justification and clear definition. This "beast" is the fantasy that virtue, our greatest joy, our deepest happiness, must be cast aside by secular grown-ups, and left in the dust to be pawed at, paraded and exploited by politicians and priests – and parents. This "beast" is the superstition that, without the tirades of parents, the bullying of gods or the guns of governments, we cannot be both rational and good.

This beast has brought down many great heroes, from Socrates to Plato to Augustine to Hume to Kant to Rand.

The cost to mankind has been enormous.

Since we have remained unable to define a rational system of universal morality, we have been forced to inflict religious horror stories on our children, or give guns, prisons and armies to a small monopoly of soulless controllers who call themselves "the state."

Since what we call "ethics" remains subjective and merely *cultural*, we inevitably end up relying on bullying, fear and violence to enforce social rules. Since ethics lack the rational basis of the scientific method, "morality" remains mired in a tribal war of bloody mythologies, each gang fighting tooth and nail for control over people's allegiance to "virtue."

We cannot live without morality, but we cannot define morality objectively – thus we remain eternally condemned to empty lives of pompous hypocrisy, cynical dominance or pious slavery.

Intellectually, there are no higher stakes in the world. Our failure to define objective and rational moral rules has cost hundreds of millions of human lives, in the wars of religions and states.

In many ways, the stakes are getting even higher.

The increased information flow of the Internet has raised the suspicions of a new generation that what is called "virtue" is nothing more – or less – than the self-serving fairy tales of their hypocritical elders. The pious lies told by those in authority – and the complicity of those who worship them – are clearer now than ever before.

"Truth" has been exposed as manipulation; "virtue" as control; "loyalty" as slavery, and what is called "morality" has been revealed as a ridiculous puppet show designed to trick weak and fearful people into enslaving themselves.

This realisation has given birth to a new generation of nihilists, just as it did in 19th century Germany. These extreme relativists reserve their most vitriolic attacks for anyone who claims any form of certainty. This postmodern generation has outgrown the cultural bigotries of their collective histories, but now view *all* truth as mere prejudicial assertion. Like wide-eyed children who have been scarred into cynical "wisdom," they view all communication as advertising, all claims as propaganda, and all moral exhortations as hypocritical thievery.

Since we have no agreement on a cohesive, objective and rational framework for evaluating moral propositions, "morality" remains mired in mysticism, and its inevitable corollary of violence. Just as, prior to the Enlightenment, religious sects warred endlessly for control over the blades of the aristocracy, so now do competing moral mythologies war for control over the state, and all its machinery of coercion.

Thus morality remains, relative to modern science, just as medieval "astronomy" did to modern astronomy – a realm of imaginary mythology, enforced through storytelling, threats, compulsion and exploitation – which actively bars any real progress towards the truth.

This "beast" of relativistic ethics looms above us, preying on us, justifying taxation, imprisonment, censorship and wars. It enslaves the young in state schools and Sunday pews; it ensnares the poor in the soft gulags of welfare; it enslaves even the unborn in the bottomless wells of national debts.

As I wrote in my previous book, "On Truth: The Tyranny of Illusion," the most fundamental lie at the centre of unproven ethical theories is that such theories are always presented to children as objective and incontrovertible facts, when in truth they are mere cultural bigotries. The reason that scientists do not need a government or a Vatican is that scientists have an objective methodology for resolving disputes: the scientific method. The reason that language does not need a central authority to guide its evolution is that it relies on the "free market" of accumulated individual preferences for style and utility.

The reason that modern morality – and morality throughout history – has always had to rely first on the bullying of children, and then on the threatening of adults, is that it is a manipulative lie masquerading as a virtuous truth.

The truth is that we need morality; the lie is that gods or governments can rationally define or justly enforce it.

My goal in this book is to define a methodology for validating moral theories that is objective, consistent, clear, rational, empirical – and *true*.

I am fully aware that, at this moment, you will very likely be feeling a rising wave of scepticism. I fully understand that the odds that some guy out there on the Internet – the homeworld of crazies – has somehow solved the philosophical problem of the ages are not particularly high – in fact, they would be so close to zero as to be virtually indistinguishable from it.

Still, not *quite* zero.

GROUND RULES

Extraordinary claims require extraordinary proof. In taking on this mammoth task – particularly in such a short book – I have set myself some basic ground rules, which are worth going over here. (Most of these will be discussed in more detail throughout the course of this book.)

1. I fully accept the Humean distinction between "is" and "ought." Valid moral rules cannot be directly derived from the existence of anything in reality. The fact that human beings in general *prefer* to live, and must successfully interact with reality in order to do so, cannot be the basis for any valid theory of ethics. Some people clearly do not prefer to live, and steadfastly reject reality, so this definition of ethics remains subjective and conditional.

2. Ethics cannot be objectively defined as "that which is good for man's survival." Certain individuals can survive very well by preying on others, so this definition of ethics does not overcome the problem of subjectivism. In biological terms, this would be analogous to describing evolutionary tendencies as "that which is good for *life's* survival" – this would make no sense. Human society is an ecosystem of competing interests, just as the rainforest is, and what is "good" for one man so often comes at the expense of another.

3. I do not believe in any "higher realm" of Ideal Forms. Morality cannot be conceived of as existing in any "other universe," either material or immaterial. If morality exists in some "other realm," it cannot then be subjected to a rigorous rational or empirical analysis – and, as Plato himself noted in "The Republic," society would thus require an elite cadre of Philosopher-Kings to communicate – or, more accurately, *enforce* – the incomprehensible edicts of this "other realm" upon everyone else. This also does not solve the problem of subjectivism, since that which is inaccessible to reason and evidence is by definition subjective.

4. I do not believe that morality can be defined or determined with reference to "arguments from effect," or the predicted consequences of ethical propositions. Utilitarianism, or "the greatest good for the greatest number," does not solve the problem of subjectivism, since the odds of any central planner knowing what is objectively good for everyone else are about the same as any central economic planner knowing how to efficiently allocate resources in the absence of price – effectively zero. Also, that which is considered "the greatest good for the greatest number" changes according to culture, knowledge, time and circumstances, which

also fails to overcome the problem of subjectivism. We do not judge the value of scientific experiments according to some Platonic higher realm, or some utilitarian optimisation – they are judged in accordance with the scientific method. I will take the same approach in this book.

5. I also refuse to define ethics as a "positive law doctrine." Although it is generally accepted that legal systems are founded upon systems of ethics, no one could argue that every law within every legal system is a perfect reflection of an ideal morality. Laws cannot directly mirror *any* objective theory of ethics, since laws are in a continual state of flux, constantly being overturned, abandoned and invented – and legal systems the world over are often in direct opposition to one another, even at the theoretical level. Sharia law is often directly opposed to Anglo-Saxon common-law, and the modern democratic "mob rule" process often seems more akin to a Mafia shootout than a sober implementation of ethical ideals.

6. I am fully open to the proposition that there is no such thing as ethics at all, and that all systems of "morality" are mere instruments of control, as Nietzsche argued so insistently. In this book, I start from the assumption that there is no such thing as ethics, and build a framework from there.

7. I do have great respect for the ethical *instincts* of mankind. The near-universal social prohibitions on murder, rape, assault and theft are facts that any rational ethicist discards at his peril. Aristotle argued that any ethical theory that can be used to prove that rape is moral must have something wrong with it, to say the least. Thus, after I have developed a framework for validating ethical theories, I run these generally accepted moral premises through that framework, to see whether or not they hold true.

8. I respect your intelligence enough to refrain from defining words like "reality," "reason," "integrity" and so on. We have enough work to do without having to reinvent the wheel.

9. Finally, I believe that any theory – especially one as fundamental as a theory of ethics – does little good if it merely confirms what everybody already knows instinctively. I have not spent years of my life working on a theory of ethics in order to run around proving that "murder is wrong." In my view, the best theories are those which verify the truths that we

all intuitively understand – and then use those principles to reveal new truths that may be completely counterintuitive.

Having spent the last few years of my life preparing, training, and then combating this beast, I hope that I have acquitted myself with some measure of honour. I believe that I have emerged victorious – though not entirely unscathed – and I look forward to seeing who shares this view. (Of course, if I have failed, I have at least failed spectacularly, which itself can be both edifying and entertaining!)

I studied the history of philosophy in graduate school, and hold a Masters degree, but I do not have a PhD in philosophy. I am far from a publicly recognized intellectual. While I may not be the *most* unlikely champion, I am also far from the most likely.

Whether I have succeeded or not is not up to you, and it is not up to me.

If the reasoning holds, the greatest beast is down.

A Modest Suggestion...

• • •

It is the height of audacity to suggest to readers how to read a book, but given the challenges of the task before us, I would like to make one small suggestion before we embark.

If we lived in the 15th century, and I were trying to convince you that the world were round, I would put forward reams of mathematical and physical proofs. If you held a contrary opinion, you would naturally react with scepticism, and be inclined to quibble with every line of proof.

However, if you and I could in fact sail around the world, and arrive back where we started without retracing our steps, you would be far more willing to accept the conceptual proofs for what you had already *experienced* to be true. You might find fault with a particular logical step or metaphor, but you would already agree with the conclusion, and thus would be more prone to help correct the details rather than reject the theory as a whole.

If my task were to respond to every possible objection to every linguistic, logical and empirical step, this book would remain forever unfinished – and unread. Perfectionism is, in essence, procrastination, and I consider the task of this book to be too important – and the dangers of false morality too grave and imminent – to spend so long trying to achieve heaven that we all end up in hell.

Thus I humbly suggest that you wait to see how effective the ethical framework I propose is at proving the most commonly accepted moral maxims of mankind before passing final judgment on the theory.

I truly believe that the definition of a rational ethical framework is the most essential task that faces mankind. I truly appreciate your interest in this crucial matter – and would like as always to thank the wonderfully kind donators who have made this work possible.

I ride into battle well armed by others.

INTRODUCTION

• • •

FOR COUNTLESS GENERATIONS, MANKIND LIVED in a kind of egocentric womb of self-imposed ignorance: the world was flat, the sun, moon and stars revolved around him, ancestors beckoned to him from beyond the mists of death, and thunder was the anger of the gods.

Burrowing out from this narcissistic womb of subjective interpretation required the labour of millennia – and cost the lives of millions. The effort required to wrench our perspective from *perceptual experience* to *conceptual logic* was terrifying, exhilarating, highly disorienting and extremely dangerous. Understanding that the world was not what it *felt like*, or *seemed like*, was – and remains – the greatest feat of our intelligence. The *truth* of reality turned out to be in the eyes of the mind, not of the flesh.

The world looks flat; it is not. The sun and the moon look the same size; they are not. The stars seem to move around the earth; they do not.

Learning the truth requires that we see the world from *outside* our senses – this does not mean a rejection of our senses, but an airtight compliance with the *real* evidence of the senses, which is not that the world is flat, but that matter, energy and physical laws are consistent. When we let go of a rock in our hand, it falls – this is the *real* evidence of the senses, not that the Earth is fixed and immovable. The idea that the world is immobile is an incorrect assumption that contradicts the direct evidence of our senses, which is that everything falls. If everything falls, the world cannot be fixed and immovable.

These are the little truths of the everyday; that rocks fall, smoke rises, fire is hot and the sun and the moon are both round. If we remain steadfastly and rigorously committed to these "little truths," we can in time derive the great truths of physics, which provide us such awesome knowledge and power.

In between the little truths and the great truths, however, are the illusions that blind us – both in physics and in ethics.

In physics, the great truths cannot contradict the little truths. No "unified field theory" can validly contradict our direct sense-experience of a falling rock or a rising flame. The greatest mathematical theory cannot be valid if applying it returns incorrect change at the checkout counter.

Historically, however, in between our own little truths and the great truths lies what I will call the "null zone."

The "Null Zone"

We tell our children not to punch each other, and we believe that violence is wrong in the abstract, as a general moral rule. The "little truth" is: *don't punch.* The "great truth" is: *violence is wrong.*

However, there exists in our minds an imaginary entity called "God," and this entity is considered perfectly moral. Unfortunately, this entity continually and grossly violates the edict that "violence is wrong" by drowning the world, consigning souls to hell despite a perfect foreknowledge of their "decisions," sanctioning rape, murder, theft, assault and other actions that we would condemn as utterly evil in any individual.

Thus we have the little truth (*don't punch*) and the great truth (*violence is wrong*) but in the middle, we have this "null zone" *where the complete opposite of both our little truths and our great truths is considered perfectly true.*

Historically, we can see the same inconsistency in physics. There are no perfect circles in our direct experience, but because of a belief in God, all planetary motion had to be a "perfect circle" – a premise that retarded astronomy for centuries. Similarly, if a man turns his head, he does not reasonably believe that the entire world rotates around him – and he would happily put this forward as not just his own "little truth," but as a *great truth*, or universal principle. Yet for most of human history, it was believed that the stars and planets rotated around the Earth, rather than that the Earth rotated. Here again we can see the "null zone" between direct sense experience and universal principle, wherein entirely opposite principles are considered to be perfectly valid.

No sane man experiences God directly. In his daily life, he fully accepts that *that which cannot be perceived does not exist*. No reasonable man flinches every time he takes a step, fearing an invisible wall that might be barring his way. The greatest abstractions of science support his approach.

Conversely, in the "null zone" of religion, the *exact opposite* of both the little truths and the great truths is believed to be true. Personally, a man believes that *that which cannot be perceived does not exist* – intellectually, science has proven this repeatedly. However, in the "null zone" of theology, the exact opposite proposition holds true – the axiom there is that *that which cannot be perceived <u>must</u> exist*.

Our belief in the virtue of the military also lies in this "null zone." If a private man is paid to murder another man, we call him a "gun for hire," and condemn him as a hit man. If, however, this man puts on a green costume with certain ribbons *and commits the same act*, we hail him as a hero and reward him with a pension. The little truth (*I should not murder*) is perfectly consistent with the great truth (*murder is wrong*) – yet in the middle there lies a "null zone," where murder magically becomes "virtuous."

If this "null zone" is valid, then no logical proposition can ever hold. If a proposition is true – and the exact opposite of that proposition is also true – then logical reasoning becomes impossible. The growth of rational science has been the steady attack upon this "null zone," and the incursion of objective consistency into these mad little pockets of subjective whim.

In old maps, before cartographers had finished their explorations, the drawings of known lands would fade into blank paper. The growth of knowledge requires first a delineation of what is not known, and then an expansion of known principles into the unknown areas.

The same is true in the realm of morality.

THE CASUALTIES

Crossing this "null zone" is fraught with peril. The road from the little truths to the great truths is paved with the bones of millions. From the death of Socrates to the torture of early scientists by religious zealots, to the millions who have murdered and died for the black fantasies of fascism and communism, any forward-thrust of human knowledge into the "null zone" is fraught with considerable danger.

Must "crossing the null zone" – or seamlessly uniting the little truths with the great truths – inevitably be so difficult and dangerous? It is an enormous challenge to unite the perceptual with the conceptual in a straight line of logical reasoning – but *must* this progress take thousands of years and oceans of blood?

If we look at the technological and economic progress of mankind, we see more or less a flat line for countless millennia, followed by massive and asymptotic spikes over the past few hundred years. It is inconceivable that some widespread genetic mutation could account for this sudden and enormous acceleration of intellectual consistency and material success. Theories claiming that a certain "snowball effect" came into existence, mysteriously propelled by an accumulation of all the little increments of knowledge that had occurred since the dawn of civilization, can usually be dismissed out of hand as entirely *ex post facto* explanations, since they have no predictive value.

If we understand that our staggering potential has been available to us for at least tens of thousands of years – and that there is both great profit and great pleasure in exercising it – then it at once becomes clear that we really *do* want to use our amazing minds.

Thus there must be a downward force that has historically acted to crush and enslave the natural liberty of mankind.

In the realm of science, it is not too hard to see the oppressive forces that continually kept our minds in near-primeval ignorance. The combination of superstition in the form of religion, and violence in the form of the aristocracy, threatened rational thinkers with intimidation, imprisonment, torture, and murder. Just as a farmer profits from the low intelligence of his cows, and a slave-owner profits from the fear of his slaves, priests and kings retained their privileges by threatening with death anyone who dared to think.

The simple truth is that "priests" and "kings" were – and are – merely men. The simple truth is that the gods and devils that were supposed to justify their rule never existed.

We have made great strides in understanding the nature and reality of simple human equality, but the sad fact of the matter is that the realm of *morality* is still lost in the "null zone" – in the destructive illusions of the "middle truths."

"Middle Truths"

Let us call the oppositional principles that reside in the "null zone" – between sense perception and conceptual consistency – the "middle truths."

These "middle truths" are the most dangerous illusions of all, because they grant the *appearance* of truth while actually *attacking* the truth.

By providing the illusion that we have found the truth, "middle truths" actually prevent us from gaining the truth. They are the last line of defense for fantasy, predation and exploitation.

Since they are not only irrational, but *anti*-rational, "middle truths" remain endlessly flexible – as long as they serve those in power. For instance, Christianity arose out of the growing fascism of the late Roman Empire partly by lashing out at the "primitive" superstitions of existing theologies. "Forget your old gods, we have a brand new God who is far better!"

"Middle truths" always take the form of a truth, followed by a lie. "Zeus is a pagan superstition" is a true statement, which was openly made by Christian proselytizers. The lie that followed was: "Yahweh is not a pagan superstition, but a real and living God."

We can personalize this a little bit more with an example that will be familiar to anyone who has ever counselled a dysfunctional friend. "My last boyfriend was a real jerk," she will say, and you will fervently agree. "My new boyfriend is really *great* though," she will add, and you will try not to roll your eyes.

It is very hard not to replace one illusion with another.

"The British government is a tyranny!" cried the American revolutionaries in the 18th century – and, after evicting the British troops, they then set up their own government and started attacking their own citizens.

"Aristocracy is an unjust abomination!" cried other revolutionaries, who then set up the tyranny of the majority in the form of democracy.

"Middle truths" can also exist in science, and similarly prevent the natural progress from the little truths to the great truths. Until the 18th century, for instance, biologists believed in "spontaneous generation," or the idea that life can spring from nonliving matter. This had never been observed, of course, but conformed to ancient writings both philosophical and religious, and so was accepted as fact. Also, prior to the Einsteinian revolution in 1905, light was believed to move through a fixed and invisible substance called "luminiferous ether," just as sound waves move through air. No scientist who believed in this theory had any empirical evidence for this "ether," either personally or scientifically – but it was considered necessary to conform to other observable characteristics.

Religion is also another "middle truth" – one of the most dangerous ones. It is true that we are a unique species in the universe, as far as we know. A giraffe is a taller quadruped, but man is not just a "smarter" primate, but something quite different. The nature of that difference remains largely unknown – the religious explanation of "we are not the same as animals because we have a soul and were created by a God" is just another example of a "middle truth." It is true that we are very different from animals. It is not true that we were created by a god and have a soul.

Just as some parasites cannot take root until they dislodge the prior parasites, "middle truths" only attack previous illusions *so that they can take their place.* Those who are sceptical of the prior fantasies are drawn towards the new fantasy. Thus does Christianity displace paganism, Marxism displace Christianity, postmodernism displace Marxism, democracy displace aristocracy, and so on.

Until the great truths are achieved, and united with the little truths, "middle truths" are just a rotating phalanx of exploitive and destructive falsehoods – specifically designed to prevent the achievement of the great truths.

And the great truths are always achieved from the little truths.

The world falls because a rock falls.

"Middle Truths" and Exploitation

Biologically, parasitism is a wholly viable survival strategy for many creatures. In the absence of ethical norms, stealing energy and resources from other creatures is perfectly sensible. In general, the most sustainable and stable form of parasitism is *symbiosis*, or mutually beneficial coexistence. Thus the bacteria that inhabit our intestines aid their own survival by helping us digest our food.

However, a virus that renders us continually exhausted, and barely able to keep ourselves alive, can scarcely be called "mutually beneficial."

If we think of our long and grim history of disaster, starvation, war, disease and poverty – and compare it with the astounding material successes of modernity – it is clear that a form of parasitism tyrannized our minds and capacities for millennia. Now that the last few hundred years have shown the power and creativity of the human spirit, we can view our species as an organism that has shaken off a terrible parasite, and sprung from an endless gasping deathbed to perform the most astounding feats of gymnastics.

When we cure ourselves of a disease, we feel better, but the disease does not. From the perspective of the smallpox virus, the smallpox vaccine is genocidal.

In the same way, the parasites that strangle mankind view the liberty of the majority with horror. Since their parasitism frees them from the demands of reality – to earn their daily bread – they inevitably view the freedom of the masses as a form of enslavement for themselves. Thus would a farmer view the "liberation" of his livestock as an utter disaster…

Establishing truth necessarily limits fantasy. Limiting fantasy necessarily limits exploitation. If I can convince you that I am a living man-God, and that the God who birthed me wants you to give me 10% of your income, or you will be punished for eternity, then I can become exceedingly rich. I am a parasite of illusions, and depend on those illusions for my sustenance as surely as fungus relies on warmth, dampness – and darkness.

Those who use moral fantasies to exploit mankind have always fought tooth and nail against those who threaten their livelihood by discovering and disseminating the truth.

We are familiar with the example of the Mafia, which threatens potential rivals with maiming and death, or the spectacle of religious sects attacking each other, or one government attacking another.

When philosophers expose the falsehoods necessary for continued exploitation, however, they are ideally not aiming to set themselves up as competitors.

They do not wish to *replace* the Mafia, or the church – they wish to eliminate it completely.

A more modern analogy would be the relationship between the state, lobbyists and taxpayers. Lobbyists will ferociously attack other lobbyists who compete for the same tax dollars. However, imagine how *all* lobbyists would band together to attack anyone who proposed eliminating the state as an institution.

Parasites will aggressively compete with one another for the host's limited resources – but it is in their best interest to band together to attack anything that threatens to eliminate the host itself.

In this way, in any society where the state and the church are nominally separated, each entity tends to compete for adherents. Where the church begins to lose ground, the state will aggressively recruit patriots – resulting in secular socialism. Where the state begins to lose ground, the church will aggressively recruit adherents – resulting in religious fundamentalism, often with tinges of libertarianism.

However, the philosophers who oppose *all* intellectual error are the sworn enemies of all the parasites that feed off illusions. The "great truths" of physics eliminate the need for supernatural agents, and render miracles impossible. The explanatory power of science wholly outshines the religious fictions that masquerade as knowledge about the physical world.

The scientific method requires that every thesis be supported by evidence and rationality. Since there is no evidence for gods – and the very *idea* of gods is innately self-contradictory – the thesis "gods exist" cannot stand. Inevitably, the religious parasites attempt to defend their thesis by trying to split reality into "two realms" – the scientific and the spiritual. However, there is no evidence for the existence of this "spiritual" realm in the present, any more than there was for the parallel universe of Platonic "Forms" 2,500 years ago.

Thus the establishment of consistent and universal truth necessarily limits and destroys the exploitive potential of illusion. In particular, the "great truths," which are universal and consistent, make redundant and ridiculous the "middle truths" – which are in fact exploitive fantasies. We are familiar with the "middle truth" of religion; a few others will be examined and revealed here, some of which may shock you.

Effective Parasitism

The most effective parasites – or viruses – are those which fool the body into indifference. Our immune systems are designed to attack foreign substances within the body, isolating and killing them. We fear HIV and cancer in particular because they are able to bypass our immune systems.

The same technique is used by intellectual parasites to disable the defense systems of those they prey upon.

If a stranger attacks you in an alley and demands your money, you will be horrified and appalled. You may fight back, you may run, or you may give him your wallet, but you would remain shocked, angry and frightened by the interaction. When you repeated the story, you would tell it in a way that reinforced the base and vile violation of your personal and property rights. Others would feel sympathy for your predicament, and would avoid said alley in the future.

This is an example of a "little truth," which is: "Stealing from me is wrong."

However, when a government agent sends you a letter demanding that you pay him money, you may feel a certain indignity, but you would not relate the story with the same horror and indignation to your friends.

This is an example of a "middle truth," which obscures a "great truth," which is that "stealing is wrong."

This book will focus on exposing and destroying these false "middle truths." I believe that mankind suffers endlessly under the tyranny of false ethical "middle truths" which justify the destructive worldviews of religious superstition, secular despotism and the cult of the family.

My thesis in this book is that in ethics, as in every other intellectual discipline, the great truths arise directly from the little truths. The disorienting fog of the "middle truths" is a hellish path to navigate, but it is worth struggling through, because the only fundamental alternative to truth is exploitation, destruction – and, inevitably, the untimely demise of millions.

Part 1: Theory

• • •

A FRAMEWORK FOR ETHICS

• • •

ETHICAL PROPOSITIONS ARE DIFFERENT FROM other types of knowledge statements. If I say, "I like jazz," that may be a true or false statement, but it is not generally considered binding upon you in any way. My preference for jazz is a mere statement of personal fondness; based on my statement, it is not incumbent upon you to either like or dislike jazz.

Similarly, if I say "I like vegetables," that is also a mere statement of personal preference. However, if I say, "vegetables are healthy food," then I have shifted from a statement of personal preference to a statement of objective fact. It is the difference between "I like ice cream," and, "Ice cream contains milk."

The fundamental difference between statements of *preference* and statements of *fact* is that statements of fact are objective, testable – and binding. If you value truth, it is incumbent upon you to accept the fact that ice cream contains milk, once it is proven. (If you do not value truth, you would never be in this debate – or any other debate – in the first place!)

If I say that the earth is round, and I provide ample proof for this statement, it is no longer up to you to determine on your own whim whether the statement is true. If I can prove that the earth is round, then you are bound to accept it as true, unless you are willing to reject reason and evidence as the criteria for truth.

If I accept the validity of mathematical laws, I cannot arbitrarily reject a mathematical proof that conforms to those laws. If I *do* reject such a proof, I can no longer claim to accept the validity of mathematical laws. My acceptance of these laws means that I am *bound* to accept as valid those proofs that conform to these laws. The rejection of a proof that conforms to rational standards is a rejection of rational standards as a whole.

The scientific method, rationality itself, and mathematical laws are all examples of *objective* criteria for establishing the truth of a proposition. It is not my opinion that two and two make four – if you also accept that two and two make four, you are not subjecting yourself to my mere opinion, but to a rational truth.

Objective Truth

A central challenge in understanding the nature of truth is the realization that "truth" does not exist in the world in the same way that a rock or tree does.

The concept "truth" is necessarily a relative term – though that does not mean a subjective or arbitrary term. The concept "health" is also a relative term – we compare "health" to sickness, and also to relative standards of health. What is considered "good health" for a 90-year-old would scarcely be considered good health for a 20-year-old. The definition of a long life is very different now than it was 500 years ago.

This does not mean, however, that the concept of "health" is entirely relative and subjective. A 10-year-old dying of leukemia is unhealthy by any definition – just as a 20-year-old marathon runner is healthy by any definition. Currently, a man who lives to 90 has statistically had a long life, though that would change if medical technology suddenly allowed us to live to be 200.

As our definition of "health" expands, it does not invalidate earlier definitions, but rather extends them. If medical technology advances to allow 90-year-olds to win marathons, then our definition of what is healthy for the aged will change – but that does not mean that the 20-year-old marathon runner suddenly becomes unhealthy. Learning algebra does not invalidate arithmetic.

Truth also has value relative to necessity as well. Newtonian physics has been supplanted by Einsteinian physics, which has proven far more accurate in extreme situations such as extraordinarily high gravity or speed. However, sailors wishing to calculate the correct path across an ocean find Newtonian physics more than accurate enough. You wouldn't want to send a spaceship to Alpha Centauri using Newtonian physics, but it is totally fine for getting a ship from Lisbon to New York. The labour involved in learning and implementing Einsteinian physics is thus a net negative for a sailor.

As a result, the sentence "Newtonian physics is less accurate than Einsteinian physics, but Newtonian physics is the best way to calculate a ship's path" can be considered a valid proposition. Newtonian physics is thus both *less accurate*, and *more appropriate*.

If we wanted to drink the purest possible water, we would likely pay thousands of dollars per bottle. Unless we were enormously rich and highly frivolous, we would never pay that much to quench our thirst. It is true that pure water is better for us, but the price that purity requires hits a threshold of diminishing returns. Thus "purer is better" gives way to "purer is worse."

Again, this does not mean that the purity of water is utterly subjective. Distilled water is always more potable than seawater.

TRUTH AND OBJECTIVE REALITY

The concept of *truth* necessarily involves the concept of *accuracy*. If I am trying to shoot an arrow at a bull's-eye, the accuracy of my shot is determined by how far my arrow lands from the centre.

What, then, is the "bull's-eye" of truth?

Well, the *truth* of a statement is measurable relative to its conformity with objective reality.

Putting aside the challenges of language for the moment, if I point to a seagull and say, "That is an anvil," I am clearly mistaken, because anvils are inorganic, and cannot fly. The truth value of my statement is measured relative to the objective facts of reality. Since the seagull is not in fact an anvil, my statement is untrue.

Naturally, this equation between truth and reality requires that language and our senses be considered relatively objective. There are many good reasons to believe that both language and sense evidence are in fact objective; we could get into a complicated discussion about this, but it should suffice to say that since you are using your eyes to read a book written in a human language, we can at least agree that your eyes, and the language we share, are at least objective enough for you to accurately process what I am writing. If they are not, we have nothing to talk about, and you haven't understood anything I've written anyway, so this sentence will be equally meaningless, and might as well have been rendered in "Wingdings":

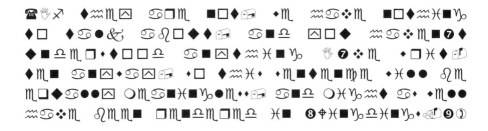

Assuming you can tell the difference between the above two fonts, we can reasonably continue.

ACCURACY AND CONSISTENCY

It is impossible for me to accurately paint a cloud, since in the time it takes to paint it, the cloud continually changes. I can accurately paint a *photograph* of a cloud, which has become frozen in time.

If I spend an hour trying to paint a cloud, and then I ask you whether or not my painting is an accurate representation of that cloud, you must necessarily reply that it is not.

In other words, where there is no consistency, there can be no accuracy.

When we dream at night, our perceptions are that the rules of "matter" and "energy" are in a constant state of flux – we are immune to gravity, and then we fly on the back of an elephant, and then we can walk through walls. It is no more possible to develop a "scientific physics of dreams" than it is to accurately paint a cloud.

Logic, science and truth, then, are impossible in the absence of *consistency*.

Fundamentally, the laws of logic are derived from the behaviour of matter and energy, at least at the perceptual level. If I tell you to throw a ball both up and down at the same time, I am asking for the impossible, which you can easily test by attempting to fulfill my request. If I tell you to plough both the north field and the south field simultaneously, you will be unable to comply. If I demand that you turn a rose into a donkey, my demand will never be met.

Perceptual reality is consistent and objective – and it is from this consistency and objectivity that we derive the laws of logic. Our statements about reality can only accurately *represent* reality as a direct result of this consistency and objectivity.

The fact that seagulls do not arbitrarily turn into anvils – or vice versa – is the root of our capacity to accurately judge the statement: "That is a seagull." If seagulls spontaneously and continually changed their nature, we would be unable to make either true or false statements regarding them – or anything for that matter.

This is the root of a key criterion of the scientific method – reproducibility. If I make a universal claim about the nature of gravity, then you should be able to reproduce that claim in your own environment. If reality were *not* consistent, then reproducibility would be an irrational criterion for the establishment of truth.

If you were a math teacher, you would be very unlikely to accept a wrong answer from a student, even if that student claimed that his answer was "right" when he wrote it down, but just somehow changed in the interim.

Thus we can accept that we must measure the validity of a statement relative to objective reality – both empirically, and logically. Logic as a discipline arises only as a result of the consistency of reality; empirical observations are also valid or invalid only as a result of the consistent nature of reality.

The Existence of "Truth"

Truth, then, can be measured according to two central criteria:

1. Truth is a measure of the correlation between the ideas in our minds and the consistency of rationality, which is directly derived from the consistent behaviour of matter and energy in the real world. (Rational consistency, or internal logic.)
2. Truth is also a measure of the correlation between the ideas in our minds and the nature and behaviour of matter and energy in the real world. (Empirical evidence, or empiricism.)

The first criterion is a measure of the consistency of ideas with themselves – and such consistency is a requirement because reality is consistent with itself. If I say, "I do not exist," that is an example of an idea that is inconsistent with itself, since I must exist in order to utter the sentence. The second criterion is a measure of the accuracy of ideas relative to empirical observations of objective reality.

Empiricism versus Rationality

Empiricism can be thought of as the ability to instinctively catch a thrown ball, or measure its movement; rationality is the ability to predict and understand the path that ball will take based on universal principles. Clearly, if balls randomly went in any and every direction – and magically transformed into flocks of doves to boot – we would be utterly unable to predict their behaviour.

Thus, since matter obeys immutable laws, our theories *about* matter must also obey immutable laws. If I know nothing about baseball, but watch a baseball game where the players always obey the rules, it would be irrational for me to formulate a theory about the rules of baseball that directly contradicted the behaviour of the players I was watching. Since the actions of the players are consistent, *any theory I develop regarding the rules that guide those actions must also be consistent.*

This requirement for consistency is one of the most basic requirements for truth. Since reality is consistent, theories regarding reality must also be consistent.

In fact, the first hurdle that any theory must overcome is that of *internal consistency.*

Internal Consistency

• • •

If I am an architect, and submit a plan to build a house, the first hurdle that I must overcome is whether or not my house can be built at all. If I submit wonderful plans for a house constructed entirely of soap bubbles, I will never get the commission, since such a "house" could never stand.

Similarly, if an engineer submits a plan for a bridge, the first criterion that must be satisfied is whether or not the bridge will stand. Other considerations such as longevity, aesthetics and so on will only apply if the bridge is physically viable to begin with.

It would be illogical – not to mention highly unproductive – to build a bridge out of random materials, using random "calculations," in order to find out whether or not it will stand. Since physical laws are consistent and universal, it is relatively easy to figure out whether or not a bridge will stand *before* building it.

There are two ways to determine the viability of the bridge before building it. The first is to look for internal inconsistencies within the premises and calculations that claim to support the viability of the bridge. If there are significant errors in the calculations justifying the weight that the bridge can support, then the bridge will likely be either over-designed, or under-designed. If erroneous mathematical calculations result in a strength of minus 50 tons per square foot at any part of the bridge, then it certainly will not stand – or, if it does, its viability will be only accidental, and not reproducible.

The mathematical calculations supporting the viability of the bridge must thus be internally consistent before any other considerations can be taken into account.

In computer terms, code that does not compile cannot be tested.

This is true in the scientific world as well. Theories are always checked for internal consistency before they are submitted to empirical tests.

The reason that internal consistency is so essential is that since theories claim to have value relative to reality, and reality is internally consistent, any theory that is *not* internally consistent cannot have value relative to reality.

Only *after* the internal consistency of the calculations has been established can the degree to which the bridge meets the specifications be reviewed. It is possible to write internally consistent specifications for a tiny bridge built entirely out of balsa wood, but unless the engineer is writing an article for a model railroading magazine, his specifications, though consistent, will fail to meet any industrial requirement.

Once we have determined that the bridge will stand, we can then determine whether or not it meets our specific needs, such as supporting the weight of pedestrians versus trains.

In the realm of economics, the same criterion applies. If my economic theory requires that prices go up and down simultaneously, then it cannot be valid, since this is impossible. Once my theory has been checked for internal consistency, I can begin to look for evidence, and/or begin using my theory to make proactive predictions.

Thus, we can see that any theory, to be valid, requires the following:

1. Internal consistency (logic).
2. External consistency (testability).

With this in mind, we can now turn to the core subject of this book.

ETHICS

• • •

SINCE ETHICS IS A SUBJECT that we all have opinions about already, it is important to outline the relationship between *instinctual* ethics and *rational* ethics.

A baseball player can catch a fly ball even if he knows nothing about physics. Similarly, we can correctly perceive an action as immoral even if we know nothing about ethical theories.

If I can catch a fly ball, then I have an instinctual *feel* for the behaviour of a baseball in flight. My instinctual understanding, however, does not give me the capacity to accurately launch a spaceship to orbit Jupiter. I have an immediate "little truth" – how the ball will move – but that does not give me a universal "great truth" – how matter behaves.

In the same way, our common moral revulsion towards actions such as rape and murder are not necessarily inaccurate, but they do not give us the capacity to create or validate consistent and empirical moral theories.

If I propose a scientific theory that completely invalidates a baseball player's ability to catch a fly ball, then I have the insurmountable challenge of explaining how the baseball player actually *does* catch the ball. Also, if my grand theory cannot accurately predict the arc of a fly ball, then I have a "great truth" which directly contradicts a "little truth," which cannot be valid. Since the necessity of logical consistency directly arises from the "little truths" of perceptual experience, any theory that directly contradicts such experience cannot be valid.

In other words, the senses give rise to logic – therefore logic cannot contradict the evidence of the senses. Evidence always trumps explanation.

In a similar manner, any valid ethical theory should be able to explain and justify our common revulsion towards crimes such as murder and rape. It cannot reasonably contradict the universal prohibitions of mankind, but must accurately incorporate and explain them.

However, just as Einsteinian physics provided surprising truths – in fact, it would have been of little value if those truths were *not* surprising – ethical theories provide the most value when they also reveal surprising truths – shocking, even. In fact, ethical theories that did not provide surprising truths would be a mere confirmation of existing instinctual preferences, and thus be of little value.

THE DISCIPLINE OF THEORETICAL ETHICS

If I say that something is "morally good" – in other words, if I propose an ethical theory – then clearly I am arguing that human beings *should* act in a particular manner, or *avoid* acting in a particular manner.

If I tell my son that he *should* become a baseball player just because I want him to, I am not stating a universal moral premise, but rather a personal preference. He is not *moral* if he becomes a baseball player, and neither is he *immoral* if he does not.

However, if I tell him that it is *moral* for sons to obey their fathers, and *immoral* for them to disobey their fathers, then I am proposing a preference that is universal, rather than merely personal – I am trying to turn a "little truth" (*I want you to become a baseball player*) into a "great truth" (*It is immoral for sons to disobey fathers*). If he wishes to be moral, he *must* become a baseball player – not because becoming a baseball player is moral, but rather because obeying his father is moral.

When I speak of a universal preference, I am really defining what is *objectively required*, or *necessary*, assuming a particular goal. *If* I want to live, I do not have to like jazz, but I *must* eat. "Eating" remains a preference – I do not *have* to eat, in the same way that I have to obey gravity – but "eating" is a universal, objective, and *binding* requirement for staying alive, since it relies on biological facts that cannot be wished away.

Ethics as a discipline can be defined as any theory regarding preferable human behaviour that is universal, objective, consistent – and binding.

Naturally, preferential behaviour can only be binding if the goal is desired. If I say that it is *preferable* for human beings to exercise and eat well, I am not saying that human beings *must not* sit on the couch and eat potato chips. What I am saying is that *if* you want to be healthy, you *should* exercise and eat well.

As Hume famously pointed out, it is impossible to derive an "ought" from an "is." What he meant by that was that *preference* in no way can be axiomatically derived from *existence*. It is true that a man who never exercises and eats poorly will be unhealthy. Does that mean that he "ought" to exercise and eat well? No. The "ought" is conditional upon the *preference*. *If* he wants to be healthy, he *ought* to exercise and eat well. It is true that if a man does not eat, he will die – we cannot logically derive from that fact a binding principle that he *ought* to eat. *If* he wants to live, then he *must* eat. However, his choice to live or not remains his own.

Similarly, there is no such thing as a universally "better" direction – it all depends upon the preferred destination. If I want to drive to New York from San Francisco, I "ought" to drive east. If I want to drive into the ocean from San Francisco, I "ought" to drive west. Neither "east" nor "west" can be considered universally "better."

It is true that very few people *do* drive into the ocean, but that does not mean that it is universally true that nobody *ought* to drive into the ocean. Principles are not democratic – or, if they are, we once more face the problem of rank subjectivism, and must throw the entire concept of ethics out the window.

"Behaviour" exists in objective reality, outside our minds – the concepts "ought," "should," and "preference," do not exist outside our minds.

However, the fact that "ought" does not exist within objective reality does not mean that "ought" is completely subjective. Neither the scientific method nor numbers themselves exist within reality either, yet science and mathematics remain objective disciplines.

SELF-DEFEATING ARGUMENTS

In order to begin our discussion of ethics, it is essential that we understand the nature of *self-defeating arguments*.

In economics, a theory cannot be valid if it requires that prices go up and down at the same time. In physics, a theory cannot be valid if it requires that gases expand and contract simultaneously. In mathematics, a theory cannot be valid if it requires that 2+2=5, since "5" is just another way of describing 2+3, not 2+2, and so to say that 2+2=5 is to say that 5=4, which is self-contradictory.

In general, any theory that contradicts itself in the utterance cannot be valid. It does not require external disproof, since it disproves itself. We do not need to examine every nook and cranny in the universe to determine that a "square circle" does not exist. The very concept is self-contradictory, and thus disproves itself in the utterance.

If I submit a complex mathematical proof to you, and you notice that, at the very beginning, I state that my proof relies on the fact that two plus two make both four and five at the same time, you do not need to read any further to know that my proof is invalid.

Similarly, as mentioned before, if I come up to you and say: "I do not exist," my thesis automatically self-destructs. If I can communicate to you that I do not exist, then clearly I exist.

If I come up to you and say: "There is no such thing as truth," then I am making a statement that I consider to be true claiming that truth does not exist. Again, my argument self-destructs.

If I tell you that "Language is meaningless," then I have also contradicted myself. In order for me to verbally communicate that language is meaningless, language must have at least some meaning.

If I tell you that "Your senses are invalid," then my argument also self-destructs, since I am using your sense of hearing to communicate to you that your sense of hearing is invalid. If I can successfully communicate my thesis to you, then your sense of hearing must be valid. Thus I must assume that your senses are valid in order to convince you that your senses are not valid, which cannot stand.

PREFERENCES

• • •

NOW THAT WE UNDERSTAND THE nature of self-defeating arguments, we can turn to the question of preferences.

Preferences are central to any methodology claiming to define the truth-value of propositions. The scientific method, for instance, is largely defined by innate preferences for logical consistency and empirical verification. For science, the premise is: *if* you want to determine a valid truth about the behaviour of matter and energy, it is *preferable* to use the scientific method.

In this sense, "preferable" does not mean "sort of better," but rather "required." *If* you want to live, it is *universally preferable* that you refrain from eating a handful of arsenic. *If* you wish to determine valid truths about reality, it is *universally preferable* that your theories be both internally consistent and empirically verifiable. "Universally preferable," then, translates to "objectively required," but we will retain the word "preferable" to differentiate between optional human absolutes and non-optional physical absolutes such as gravity.

Similarly, if ethical theories can be at all valid, then they must *at least* be both internally and externally consistent. In other words, an ethical theory that contradicts itself cannot be valid – and an ethical theory that contradicts empirical evidence and near-universal preferences also cannot be valid.

Thus in ethics, just as in science, mathematics, engineering and all other disciplines that compare theories to reality, *valid theories must be both logically consistent and empirically verifiable.*

PREFERENCES AND EXISTENCE

If I say "I like ice cream," only one word remains ambiguous in that sentence. Clearly "I" exist, since I am expressing a personal preference. Equally clearly, "ice cream" also exists in reality. However, the word "like" is more problematic.

Preferences do not exist objectively within reality. If you were obsessively curious, you could perhaps follow me around and record every time I ate ice cream, which would probably provide a good empirical basis for establishing my preference for it. The possibility could exist, however, that I am in fact a masochist, and dislike ice cream intensely, and prefer to torture myself with its unpleasant taste – and then confuse you by claiming to like it.

We can find *evidence* for preferences; we cannot find preference *itself* in reality. Preference exists as a *relationship* between consciousness and matter, just as gravity exists as a relationship between bodies of mass.

Putting aside the challenging questions of free will versus determinism, it is reasonable to assume that whatever a person is doing in the present is what he or she "prefers" to do. If I get up and go to work, then obviously I *prefer* to do that, as opposed to all other alternatives. Even if I hate my job, I clearly hate it *less* than, say, being penniless.

Given that human beings can perform a near infinite variety of actions, whatever a person is doing in the moment is chosen out of all other possible options. I am choosing to write this book rather than, say, learning how to tango.

When we apply this simple fact to ethical arguments, we come up with some very interesting results.

PREFERENCES AND ARGUMENTS

Remembering our above analysis of self-defeating arguments, we can easily understand the contradictory nature of the statement: "preferences do not exist." Given that every human action – including making philosophical statements – is chosen in preference to every other possible action, arguing that preferences do not exist requires a *preference* for arguing that preferences do not exist, which is a self-contradictory statement.

Arguing that preferences do not exist is exactly the same as arguing that language does not exist. It is an utterly self-defeating argument.

Since it is impossible to act without expressing a preference – either implicitly or explicitly – anyone who acts accepts the premise that preferences exist. Thus it is impossible to debate the existence of preferences without accepting the existence of preferences.

PREFERENCES AND UNIVERSALITY

The next question thus becomes: are preferences purely subjective, or can they be universal?

Clearly, some preferences are subjective. Musical tastes, personal hobbies, favourite literature and so on are all subjective and personal preferences.

The challenge arises when we try to define some preferences as *objective*.

The proposition before us is thus: *can some preferences be objective, i.e. universal?*

When I say that some preferences may be objective, I do not mean that all people follow these preferences at all times. If I were to argue that *breathing* is an objective preference, I could be easily countered by the example of those who commit suicide by hanging themselves. If I were to argue that eating is an objective preference, my argument could be countered with examples of hunger strikes and anorexia.

Thus when I talk about universal preferences, I am talking about what people *should* prefer, not what they always *do* prefer. To use a scientific analogy, to truly understand the universe, people *should* use the scientific method – this does not mean that they always do so, since clearly billions of people consult ancient fairy tales rather than modern science for "answers." There is no way to achieve truth about the universe without science, but people are perfectly free to redefine "truth" as "error," and content themselves with mystical nonsense.

Likewise, if a man wants to cure an infection, he *should* take antibiotics rather than perform an Aztec rain dance. The preference for taking antibiotics rather than doing a rain dance is universal, since dancing cannot cure infections. Thus, although there is the occasional madman who will try to cure himself through dancing, it is still *universally preferable* that if a man wants to cure himself, he must take antibiotics.

In other words, if you want to get to the top of a mountain, wishing for it will never work. If you want to know the origins of the universe, prayer will never provide an answer. People still wish, and pray, but that does not make wishing or praying any more effective.

With that in mind, let us turn to the question of whether or not universal preferences can be valid.

Arguments and Universality
If I choose to debate, I have implicitly accepted a wide variety of premises that are worth spending some time to unpack here.

Premise 1: We Both Exist
If I choose to debate with you, then I necessarily must accept that we both exist. If I believe that I exist, but you do not, then debating makes no sense, and would be the action of a madman. If I were to start arguing with my reflection in a mirror, I should be sedated, not debated.

PREMISE 2: THE SENSES HAVE THE CAPACITY FOR ACCURACY

Since human beings cannot communicate psychically, all debates necessarily involve the evidence of the senses. Writing presupposes sight; talking requires hearing; Braille requires touch. Thus any proposition that depends upon the invalidity of the senses automatically self-destructs.

PREMISE 3: LANGUAGE HAS THE CAPACITY FOR MEANING

Similar to Premise 2, since all arguments require language, any proposition that rests on the premise that language is meaningless is immediately disproven. Using language to argue that language has no meaning is like using a courier to send a message arguing that couriers never deliver messages.

PREMISE 4: CORRECTION REQUIRES UNIVERSAL PREFERENCES

If you correct me on an error that I have made, you are implicitly accepting the fact that it would be *better* for me to correct my error. Your preference for me to correct my error is not subjective, but objective, and universal.

You don't say to me: "You should change your opinion to mine because *I* would prefer it," but rather: "You should correct your opinion because it is objectively incorrect." My error does not arise from merely disagreeing with you, but as a result of my deviance from an objective standard of truth. Your argument that I should correct my false opinion rests on the objective value of truth – i.e. that truth is *universally preferable* to error, and that truth is *universally objective*.

PREMISE 5: AN OBJECTIVE METHODOLOGY EXISTS FOR SEPARATING TRUTH FROM FALSEHOOD

If you disagree with me, but I tell you that you must agree with me because I am always right, it is unlikely that you would be satisfied by the rigor of my argument. If you provided good reasons as to why I was wrong, but I just kept repeating that I was right because I am *always* right, our interaction could scarcely be categorized as a debate.

The moment that I provide some sort of objective criterion for determining truth from falsehood, I am accepting that truth is more than a matter of opinion.

This does not necessarily mean that my objective criteria are *logical* – I could refer you to a religious text, for example. However, even if I do so, I am still accepting that the truth is something that is arrived at independent of mere personal assertion – that an objective methodology exists for separating truth from falsehood.

Premise 6: Truth Is Better Than Falsehood

If I tell you that the world is flat, and you reply that the world is not flat, but round, then you are implicitly accepting the axiom that truth and falsehood both exist objectively, and that truth is better than falsehood.

If I tell you that I like chocolate ice cream, and you tell me that you like vanilla, it is impossible to "prove" that vanilla is objectively better than chocolate. The moment that you correct me with reference to objective *facts*, you are accepting that objective facts exist, and that objective truth is *universally preferable* to subjective error.

Premise 7: Peaceful Debating is the Best Way to Resolve Disputes

If I tell you that the world is flat, and you pull out a gun and shoot me, this would scarcely be an example of a productive debate. True, our disagreement would have been "resolved" – but because only one of us was left standing at the end.

If you told me in advance that you would deal with any disagreement by shooting me, I would be unlikely to engage in a debate with you.

Thus it is clear that any debate relies on the implicit premise that evidence, reason, truth and objectivity are the *universally preferable* methods of resolving disputes between individuals. It would be completely illogical to argue that differences of opinion should be resolved through the use of violence – the only consistent argument for the *value* of violence is the *use* of violence. (It will be useful to keep this particular premise in mind, since it will be very important later on.)

In essence, then, debating requires an objective methodology, through meaningful language, in the pursuit of universal truth, which is objectively preferable to personal error.

This preference for universal truth is not a preference of *degree*, but of *kind*. A shortcut that reduces your driving time by half is twice as good as a longer route – but both are *infinitely preferable* to driving in the completely wrong direction.

In the same way, the truth is not just "better" than error – it is *infinitely preferable*, or *required*.

PREMISE 8: INDIVIDUALS ARE RESPONSIBLE FOR THEIR ACTIONS

If I argue that human beings are not responsible for their actions, I am caught in a paradox, which is the question of *whether or not I am responsible for my argument*, and also *whether or not you are responsible for your response.*

If my argument that human beings are *not* responsible for their actions is true, then I am not responsible for my argument, and you are not responsible for your reply. However, if I believe that you are not responsible for your reply, it would make precious little sense to advance an argument – it would be exactly the same as arguing with a television set. (The question of responsibility is, of course, closely related to the question of free will versus determinism, which will be the subject of another book.)

Thus, fundamentally, if I tell you that you are not responsible for your actions, I am telling you that it is universally preferable for you to believe that preference is impossible, since if you have no control over your actions, you cannot choose a preferred state, i.e. truth over falsehood. Thus this argument, like the above arguments, self-destructs.

Universally Preferable Behaviour

• • •

As a result of the above arguments, we can see that it is impossible to enter into any debate without accepting the premise that certain behaviours are *universally preferable*.

I use the word "behaviour" here rather than "thought" because it is important to differentiate between purely internal and unverifiable states such as "thinking" from objective and verifiable states such as "acting," "writing" and "speaking."

It is impossible to prove that I dreamt of an elephant last night. It *is* possible to prove that I have written the word "elephant," which is why I use the word "behaviour" rather than "thought."

Acquiescing to superior logic in an argument is an *action*. If, every time I conceded a point to you, I said nothing, but rather just stared at you blankly, you would find it rather irritating to debate me. To concede a point, I must perform the action of verbal acquiescence.

Thus it can be seen that, inherent in the very act of arguing are a number of embedded premises that cannot be conceivably overturned.

If I ask you to meet me on the tennis court, and show up with a hunting rifle, we may end up playing a sport of sorts, but it certainly will not be tennis. When I ask you to meet me on the tennis court for a game, implicit in that request is an acceptance of the rules of tennis.

Historically, those engaged in ethical debating have often failed to maintain this basic reality.

I cannot submit a scientific paper written in my own personal language, claiming that it has been refereed by my psychic goldfish, and expect to be taken seriously. Similarly, I cannot start a philosophical debate on ethics with reference to my own personal values, and claim that my arguments have all been validated by Trixie the omniscient and invisible leprechaun, and expect to be taken seriously.

The very act of debating requires an acceptance of universally preferable behaviour (UPB). There is no way to rationally respond to an ethical argument *without* exhibiting UPB.

Let us now turn to a series of positive proofs for UPB.

UPB AND VALIDITY

One of the central challenges faced by modern philosophers is the need to prove that moral rules are both possible and universal. Until moral rules can be subjected to the same rigour and logic as any other propositions, we will forever be stymied by subjectivism, political prejudices and the pragmatic "argument from effect."

The closest historical analogy to our present situation occurred in the 15th and 16th centuries, during the rise of the scientific method. The early pioneers who advocated a rational and empirical approach to knowledge faced the same prejudices that we face today – all the same irrationalities, entrenched powers of church and state, mystical and subjective "absolutes" and early educational barriers. Those who advocated the primacy of rationality and empirical observation over Biblical fundamentalism and secular tyrannies faced the determined opposition of those wielding both cross and sword. Many were tortured to death for their intellectual honesty – we face far less risk, and so should be far more courageous in advocating what is *true* over what is *believed*.

In order to attack false moralities, we must start from the beginning, just as the first scientists did. Francis Bacon did not argue that the scientific method was more "efficient" than prayer, Bible texts or starvation-induced visions. He simply said that if we want to understand nature, we must observe nature and theorize logically – and that there is *no other* route to knowledge.

We must take the same approach in defining and communicating *morality*. We must begin using the power and legitimacy of the scientific method to prove the validity and universality of moral laws. We must start from the beginning, build logically and reject *any* irrational or non-empirical substitutes for the truth.

What does this look like in practice? All we have to do is establish the following axioms:

- Morality is a valid concept.
- Moral rules must be consistent for all mankind.
- The validity of a moral theory is judged by its consistency.

To start from the very beginning… are moral rules – or universally preferable human behaviours – valid at all?

There are only two possibilities when it comes to moral rules, just as there are in any logical science. Either universal moral rules are valid, or they are not. (In physics, the question is: either universal physical rules are valid, or they are not.)

A rule can be valid if it *exists empirically*, like gravity, or because it is *true*, like the equation 2+2=4.

We must then first ask: do moral rules exist at all?

Certainly not in material reality, which does not contain or obey a single moral rule. Moral rules are different from the rules of physics, just as the scientific method is different from gravity. Matter innately obeys gravity or the second law of thermodynamics, but "thou shalt not murder" is nowhere inscribed in the nature of things. Physical laws *describe* the behaviour of matter, but do not contain a single *prescription*. Science says that matter *does* behave in a certain manner – never that it *should* behave in a certain manner. A theory of gravity proves that if you push a man off a cliff, he will fall. It will not tell you whether you *should* push him or not.

Thus it cannot be said that moral rules exist in material reality, and neither are they automatically obeyed like the laws of physics – which does *not* mean that moral laws are false, subjective or irrelevant. The scientific method itself does not exist in reality either – and is also optional – but it is not at all false, subjective or irrelevant.

If we can prove that moral theories can be objective, rational and verifiable, this will provide the same benefits to ethics that subjecting *physical* theories to the scientific method did.

Before the rise of the scientific method, people believed that matter obeyed the subjective whims of gods and devils – and people believe the same of morality now. Volcanoes erupted because the mountain-god was angry; good harvests resulted from human or animal sacrifices. No one believed that absolute physical laws could limit the will of the gods – and so science could never develop. Those who histori-cally profited from defining physical reality as subjective – mostly priests and aris-tocrats – fought the subjugation of physical theories to the scientific method, just as those who currently profit from defining morality as subjective – mostly priests and politicians – currently fight the subjugation of *moral* theories to objective and universal principles.

As mentioned above, the scientific method is essentially a methodology for separating accurate from inaccurate theories by subjecting them to two central tests: logical consistency and empirical observation – and by always subjugating logical consistency to empirical observation. If I propose a perfectly consistent and logical theory that says that a rock will float *up* when thrown off a cliff, any empirical test proves my theory incorrect, since observation always trumps hypothesis.

A further aspect of the scientific method is the belief that, since matter is com-posed of combinations of atoms with common, stable and predictable proper-ties, the behaviour of matter must also be common, stable and predictable. Thus experiments must be *reproducible* in different locations and times. I cannot say that my "rock floating" theory is correct for just one particular rock, or on the day I first tested it, or at a single location. My theories must describe the behaviour of *matter*, which is universal, common, stable and predictable.

Finally, there is a generally accepted rule – sometimes called Occam's Razor – which states that, of any two theories that have the same predictive power, the simpler of the two is preferable. Prior to the Copernican revolution, when Earth was considered the centre of the universe, the retrograde motion of Mars when Earth passed it in orbit around the sun caused enormous problems to the Ptolemaic system of astronomical calculations. "Circles within circles" multiplied enormously, which were all cleared away by simply placing the sun at the centre of the solar system and accepting the elliptical nature of planetary orbits.

Thus any valid scientific theory must be (a) universal, (b) logical, (c) empirically verifiable, (d) reproducible and (e) as simple as possible.

The methodology for judging and proving a *moral* theory is exactly the same as the methodology for judging and proving any other theory.

Moral Rules: A Definition
The first question regarding moral rules is: *what are they?*

Simply put, *morals* are a set of rules claiming to accurately and consistently identify universally preferable human behaviours, just as *physics* is a set of rules claiming to accurately and consistently identify the universal behaviour of matter.

The second question to be asked is: is there any such thing as "universally preferable behaviour" at all? If there is, we can begin to explore what such behaviour might be. If not, then our examination must stop here – just as the examination of Ptolemaic astronomy ceased after it became commonly accepted that the Sun was in fact the centre of the solar system.

UPB: FIVE PROOFS

As we discussed above, the proposition that *there is no such thing as preferable behaviour* contains an insurmountable number of logical and empirical problems. "Universally preferable behaviour" *must* be a valid concept, for five main reasons.

The first is logical: if I argue *against* the proposition that universally preferable behaviour is valid, I have already shown my preference for truth over falsehood – as well as a preference for correcting those who speak falsely. Saying that there is no such thing as universally preferable behaviour is like shouting in someone's ear that sound does not exist – it is innately self-contradictory. In other words, if there is *no such thing* as universally preferable behaviour, then one *should* oppose anyone who claims that there *is* such a thing as universally preferable behaviour. However, if one "should" do something, then one has just created universally preferable behaviour. Thus universally preferable behaviour – or moral rules – must be valid.

Syllogistically, this is:

1. The proposition is: the concept "universally preferable behaviour" must be valid.
2. Arguing against the validity of universally preferable behaviour demonstrates universally preferable behaviour.
3. Therefore no argument against the validity of universally preferable behaviour can be valid.

We all know that there are subjective preferences, such as liking ice cream or jazz, which are not considered binding upon other people. On the other hand, there are other preferences, such as rape and murder, which clearly *are* inflicted on others. There are also preferences for logic, truth and evidence, which are also binding upon others (although they are not usually violently inflicted) insofar as we all accept that an illogical proposition must be false or invalid.

Those preferences which can be considered binding upon others can be termed "universal preferences," or "moral rules."

How else can we know that the concept of "moral rules" is valid?

We can examine the question biologically as well as syllogistically.

For instance, all matter is subject to physical rules – and everything that lives is in addition subject to certain requirements, and thus, if it is alive, must have followed universally preferred behaviours. Life, for instance, requires fuel and oxygen. Any living mind, of course, is an organic part of the physical world, and so is subject to physical laws and must have followed universally preferred behaviours – to argue otherwise would require proof that consciousness is not composed of matter, and is not organic – an impossibility, since it has mass, energy, and life. Arguing that consciousness is subject to neither physical rules nor universally preferred behaviours would be like arguing that human beings are immune to gravity, and can flourish without eating.

Thus it is impossible that anyone can logically argue against universally preferable behaviour, since if he is alive to argue, he must have followed universally preferred behaviours such as breathing, eating and drinking.

Syllogistically, this is:

1. All organisms require universally preferred behaviour to live.
2. Man is a living organism.
3. Therefore all living men are alive due to the practice of universally preferred behaviour.
4. Therefore any argument against universally preferable behaviour requires an acceptance and practice of universally preferred behaviour.
5. Therefore no argument against the existence of universally preferable behaviour can be valid.

Since the scientific method requires empirical corroboration, we must also look to reality to confirm our hypothesis – and here the validity of universally preferable behaviour is fully supported.

Every sane human being believes in moral rules of some kind. There is some disagreement about what *constitutes* moral rules, but everyone is certain that moral rules are valid – just as many scientists disagree, but all scientists accept the validity of the scientific method itself. One can argue that the Earth is round and not flat – which is analogous to changing the definition of morality – but one cannot argue that the Earth does not exist at all – which is like arguing that there is no such thing as universally preferable behaviour.

Or:

1. For a scientific theory to be valid, it must be supported by empirical observation.
2. If the concept of "universally preferable behaviour" is valid, then mankind should believe in universally preferable behaviour.
3. All men believe in universally preferable behaviour.
4. Therefore empirical evidence exists to support the validity of universally preferable behaviour – and the existence of such evidence *opposes* the proposition that universally preferable behaviour is not valid.

The fourth argument for the validity of universally preferable behaviour is also empirical. Since human beings have an almost-infinite number of choices to make in life, to say that there are no principles of universally preferable behaviour would be to say that all choices are equal (i.e. subjective). However, all choices are *not* equal, either logically or through empirical observation.

For instance, if food is available, almost all human beings prefer to eat every day. When cold, almost all human beings seek warmth. Almost all parents choose to feed, shelter and educate their children. There are many examples of common choices among humankind, which indicate that universally preferable behaviour abounds and is part of human nature.

As mentioned above, no valid theory of physics can repudiate the simple fact that children can catch fly-balls – in the same way, no valid theory of ethics can reject the endless evidence for the acceptance of UPB.

Or:

1. Choices are almost infinite.
2. Most human beings make very similar choices.
3. Therefore not all choices can be equal.
4. Therefore universally preferable choices must be valid.

The fifth argument for the validity of universally preferable behaviour is evolutionary.

Since all organic life requires preferential behaviour to survive, we can assume that those organisms which make the most successful choices are the ones most often selected for survival.

Since man is the most successful species, and man's most distinctive organ is his mind, it must be man's *mind* that has aided him the most in making successful choices. The mind itself, then, has been selected as successful by its very ability to make successful choices. Since the human mind only exists as a *result* of choosing universally preferable behaviour, universally preferable behaviour must be a valid concept.

Or:

1. Organisms succeed by acting upon universally preferable behaviour.
2. Man is the most successful organism.
3. Therefore man must have acted most successfully on the basis of universally preferable behaviour.
4. Man's mind is his most distinctive organ.
5. Therefore man's mind must have acted most successfully on the basis of universally preferable behaviour.
6. Therefore universally preferable behaviour must be valid.

We could bring many more arguments to support the existence and validity of UPB, but we shall rest our case with the above, and move to an examination of the nature of UPB.

UPB: Optional and Objective

Since we have proven the validity of universally preferable behaviour, the question of morality now shifts. Since morality *is* valid, what theories can quantify, classify, explain and predict it?

First of all, we must remember that morality is clearly optional. Every man is subject to gravity and requires food to live, but no man has to act morally. If I rape, steal or kill, no thunderbolt strikes me down. Moral rules, like the scientific method or biological classifications, are merely ways of rationally organizing facts and principles relative to objective reality.

The fact that compliance with moral rules is *optional*, however, has confused many thinkers into believing that morality itself is *subjective.*

Nothing could be further from the truth.

Living organisms are part of material reality, and material reality is rational and objective. Applying moral theories is optional, but that does not mean that all moral theories are subjective. The scientific method is also optional, but it is not subjective. Applying biological classifications is optional, but biology is not subjective. Choices are optional; consequences are not. I can choose not to eat, but I cannot choose to live without eating. I can choose to behead someone, but I cannot choose whether or not they can live without a head. Morality is thus optional, but the *effects* of moral choices are measurable and objective.

Now, since morality is a valid concept, the next question is: to what degree or extent is morality valid?

As mentioned above, the first test of any scientific theory is *universality.* Just as a theory of physics must apply to *all* matter, a moral theory that claims to describe the preferable actions of mankind *must apply to all mankind.* No moral theory can be valid if it argues that a certain action is *right* in Syria, but *wrong* in San Francisco. It cannot say that Person A *must* do X, but Person B must *never* do X. It cannot say that what was *wrong* yesterday is *right* today – or vice versa. If it does, it is false and must be refined or discarded.

To be valid, any moral theory must also pass the criterion of *logical consistency*. Since the behaviour of matter is logical, consistent and predictable, all theories involving matter – either organic or inorganic – must also be logical, consistent and predictable. The theory of relativity cannot argue that the speed of light is both constant and not constant at the same time, or that it is 186,000 miles per second, five fathoms in depth and also green in colour.

However, since moral theories apply to mankind, and mankind is organic, the degree of *empirical* consistency required for moral theories is less than that required for *inorganic* theories. All rocks, for instance, must fall down, but not all horses have to be born with only one head. Biology includes three forms of "randomness," which are environment, genetic mutation and free will. For example, poodles are generally friendly, but if beaten for years, will likely become aggressive. Horses are defined as having only one head, but occasionally, a two-headed mutant is born. Similarly, human beings generally prefer eating to starving – except anorexics. These exceptions do not bring down the entire science of biology. Thus, since moral theories describe mankind, they cannot be subjected to exactly the same requirements for consistency as theories describing inorganic matter.

The final test that any moral theory must pass is the criterion of empirical observation. For instance, a moral theory must explain the universal prevalence of moral beliefs among mankind, as well as the divergent results of human moral "experiments" such as fascism, communism, socialism or capitalism. It must also explain some basic facts about human society, such as the fact that state power always increases, or that propaganda tends to increase as state power increases. If it fails to explain the past, understand the present and predict the future, then it must be rejected as invalid.

UPB: The Practice
How does all this look in practice? Let's look at how the requirement for *universality* affects moral theories. We shall touch here on proofs and disproofs for specific moral propositions, which we shall examine in more detail in Part 2.

If I say that gravity affects matter, it must affect *all* matter. If even one pebble proves immune to gravity, my theory is in trouble. If I propose a moral theory that argues that people should not murder, it must be applicable to *all* people. If certain people (such as soldiers) are exempt from that rule, then I have to either prove that soldiers are *not* people, or accept that my moral theory is false. There is no other possibility. On the other hand, if I propose a moral theory that argues that all people *should* murder, then I have saved certain soldiers, but condemned to evil all those *not* currently murdering someone (including those being murdered!) – which is surely incorrect.

If, to save the virtue of soldiers, I alter my theory to argue that it is moral for people to murder if someone else tells them to (a political leader, say), then I must deal with the problem of universality. If Politician A can order a soldier to murder an Iraqi, then the Iraqi must also be able to order the soldier to murder Politician A, and the soldier can also order Politician A to murder the Iraqi. The application of this theory results in a general and amoral paralysis, and thus is proven invalid.

I also cannot logically argue that is wrong for *some* people to murder, but right for *other* people to murder. Since all human beings share common physical properties and requirements, proposing one rule for one person and the *opposite* rule for another is invalid – it is like proposing a physics theory that says that some rocks fall down, while others fall up. Not only is it illogical, it contradicts an observable fact of reality, which is that human beings as a species share common character-istics, and so cannot be subjected to opposing rules. Biologists have no problems classifying certain organisms as "human" because they share common and easily identifiable characteristics – it is only moralists who seem to find this level of con-sistency impossible.

Furthermore, if my moral theory "proves" that the *same man* should not murder one day, but *should* murder the next day (say, when he steps out into the Iraqi des-ert), then my position is even more ludicrous. That would be equivalent to arguing that *one day a rock falls downward, and the next day it falls upward!* To call this any kind of consistent theory is to make madness sanity.

Since valid theories require *logical consistency*, a moral theory cannot be valid if it is both true and false at the same time. A moral theory that approves of stealing, for instance, faces an insurmountable logical problem. No moral theory should, if it is universally applied, directly eliminate behaviour it defines as moral while simultaneously creating behaviour it defines as *immoral*. If everyone *should* steal, then no one *will* steal – which means that the moral theory can never be practiced. And *why* will no one steal? Well, because a man will only steal if he can *keep* the property he is stealing. He's not going to bother stealing a wallet if someone else is going to immediately steal that wallet from him.

Any moral theory proposing that "stealing is good" is also automatically invalid because it posits that property rights are both valid and invalid *at the same time*, and so fails the test of logical consistency. If I steal from you, I am saying that *your* property rights are invalid. However, I want to *keep* what I am stealing – and therefore I am saying that *my* property rights are valid. However, property rights cannot be both valid and invalid at the same time, and so this proposition itself must be invalid.

Similarly, any moral theory that advocates rape faces a similar contradiction. Rape can *never* be moral, since any principle that approves it automatically contradicts itself. If rape is justified on the principle that "taking pleasure is always good," then such a principle immediately fails the test of logical consistency, since the rapist may be "taking pleasure," but his victim certainly is *not*. (The same goes, of course, for murder and assault. We will be returning to these proofs – as well as a further examination of property rights – in more detail in Part 2 of this book.)

Thus subjecting moral theories to the scientific method produces results that conform to rationality, empirical observations and plain common sense. Murder, theft, arson, rape and assault are all proven immoral. (Universal and positive moral rules can also be proven – i.e. the universal validity of property rights and non-violence – but we shall discuss that in Part 2.)

To aid in swallowing this rather large conceptual pill, below is a table that helps equate theories of physics and biology with scientific theories of universally preferable (or moral) behaviour:

	Physics	Biology	Morality
Subject	Matter	Organic Matter	Preferable behaviour for mankind
Instance	A rock	A horse	A man
Sample Rule	Gravity	The desire for survival	Self-ownership
Sample Theory	Entropy	Evolution	Property rights
Sample Classification	Matter/Energy	Reptile/Mammal	Good/Evil
Example	Matter cannot be created or destroyed, merely converted to energy and back.	If it is alive and warm-blooded, it is a mammal.	Stealing is wrong.
Hypothesis	Atoms share common structures and properties, and so behave in predictable and consistent manners.	Organic matter has rules – or requirements – that are common across classifications.	Universally preferable behaviour shares common rules and requirements.
Proof	Logical consistency, empirical verification.	Logical consistency, empirical verification.	Logical consistency, empirical verification.
Negative Proof Example	If mass does not attract mass, theories relying on gravity are incorrect	If organisms do not naturally self-select for survival, the theory of evolution is incorrect.	If communism succeeds relative to its stated goals, theories based on the universal validity of property rights are incorrect.

In conclusion, it is safe to say that (a) moral rules are valid, and (b) moral theories must be subjected to the rigours of logic and evidence, just as theories of physics and biology are. Any moral theory based on non-universal or self-contradictory principles is demonstrably false.

UPB: The Framework

UPB can thus be seen as a framework for validating ethical theories or propositions – just as the scientific method is a framework that is used to validate scientific theories or propositions.

An example of a moral proposition is: "the initiation of the use of force is wrong." UPB is the methodology that tests that proposition against both internal consistency and empirical observation. UPB thus first asks: *is the proposition logical and consistent?* UPB then asks: *what evidence exists for the truth of the proposition?*

To keep this book at a reasonable length, we will in general deal mostly with the first criterion of logical consistency. For the second criterion, we shall rely for evidence on the universal prohibitions across all cultures against certain actions such as rape, theft, assault and murder. Much more could be written on the historical evidence that helps support or reject various moral propositions, but we shall leave that for another time. If we establish the validity of UPB, we have achieved an enormous amount. If we do not, evidence will scarcely help us.

Let us now turn to the question of whether the UPB framework deals with matters of *ethics*, or *aesthetics*, or both.

UPB: Ethics or Aesthetics?

• • •

IN GENERAL, WE WILL USE the term *aesthetics* to refer to non-enforceable preferences – universal or personal – while *ethics* or *morality* will refer to enforceable preferences. It is *universally preferable* (i.e. required) to use the scientific method to validate physical theories, but we cannot use force to *inflict* the scientific method on those who do not use it, since *not using the scientific method is not a violent action.*

Non-violent actions by their very nature are *avoidable.* If a physicist stops using the scientific method, but instead starts consulting tarot cards, he is not violently inflicting his choice on me, and I can avoid him. A rapist, on the other hand, is violently inflicting his preferences upon his victim.

Although we first focused on UPB in the realm of ethics, UPB can now be seen as an "umbrella term," which includes such disciplines as:

- The scientific method
- Logic
- Empiricism
- Debating
- Language
- Ethics

Ethics is the subset of UPB which deals with *inflicted* behaviour, or the use of violence. Any theory that justifies or denies the use of violence is a *moral* theory, and is subject to the requirements of logical consistency and empirical evidence.

Let us look at three actions, to help us further distinguish between ethics and aesthetics. The first action is *irrationality*; the second is *lying*; the third is *murder*. (Please note that the examples below are not proofs, but rather situations that a valid ethical theory should be able to encompass and explain. We will get to the actual proofs shortly.)

IRRATIONALITY

Let's say that you and I are having a debate about the existence of God. After I put forth my arguments, you clap your hands over your ears, singing out that God is telling you that He exists, and therefore all of my arguments mean nothing. Clearly, your response to my position is irrational. However annoying I might find your behaviour, though, it would scarcely seem reasonable for me to vent my frustration by pulling out a gun and shooting you. I believe that it is *universally preferable* to use logic and evidence rather than rely on voices in our heads, but this universal preference is not reasonably enforceable in the *physical* sense, through violence or the threat thereof.

LYING

Let's say that you and I set the rules for a debate, and we both agree to judge the question of the existence of God according to reason and evidence. If, as the debate continues, you fall back to a position of blind faith, and reject my arguments *despite* their rationality and evidence, you are not keeping your word. In other words, you were lying when you said that the question would be decided by reason and evidence.

The difference between these two situations (irrationality versus lying) is the difference between a contractual and a non-contractual arrangement. If I hand you $100 and then walk away, I cannot justly come up to you in a year and say that you now owe me $100, because it was a loan. If, on the other hand, you agree to pay me back the money in a year, and then fail to do so, that is quite a different situation.

In the example of "lying," although you have clearly broken your word, and wasted my time, it would not seem to be either moral or reasonable for me to pull out a gun and shoot you.

A reasonable moral theory should be able to explain why this is the case.

MURDER

If you rush at me with a knife raised, few people would argue with my right to defend myself. If shooting you were the only way that I could reasonably ensure my own safety, it would generally be considered a regrettable necessity.

REQUIREMENTS FOR ETHICS

Certain preconditions must exist, or be accepted, in order for ethical judgments or theories to have any validity or applicability. Clearly, choice and personal responsibility must both be accepted as axioms. If a rock comes bouncing down a hill and crashes into your car, we do not hold the rock morally responsible, since it has no consciousness, cannot choose, and therefore cannot possess personal responsibility. If the rock dislodged simply as a result of time and geology, then no one is responsible for the resulting harm to your car. If, however, you saw me push the rock out of its position, you would not blame the rock, but rather me. To add a further complication, if it turns out that I dislodged the rock because another man forced me to at gunpoint, you would be far more likely to blame the gun-toting initiator of the situation rather than me.

As we have discussed above, entering into any debate requires an acceptance of the realities of choice, values and personal responsibility.

However, these factors are also present in the choice of the color of paint for a room, yet we would scarcely say that selecting a hue is a *moral* choice. Thus there must be other criteria which must be present in order for a choice or proposition to be moral.

We all have preferences – from the merely personal ("I like ice cream") to the socially preferable ("It is good to be on time") to universal morality ("Thou shalt not murder").

There is little point writing a book about personal preferences – and we can turn to Ann Landers for a discussion of socially preferable behaviour – here, then, we will focus on the possibility of *Universally Preferable Behaviour.*

CHOICE

If I accept your invitation to a dinner party, but find the conversation highly offensive, I can decide to get up and leave – and I can also choose to never accept another invitation from you. This capacity for escape and/or avoidance is an essential characteristic differentiating *aesthetics* from *ethics*.

If, however, when I decide to leave your dinner party, you leap up and chain me to my chair, clearly I no longer have the free choice to leave. This is the moment at which your rudeness becomes overt aggression, and crosses the line from aesthetics to ethics.

If, after vowing monogamy, I cheat on my wife, and she decides to leave me, I have certainly done her wrong, but the wrong that I have done by cheating would be very different from the wrong I would do if I lock her in the basement to prevent her from leaving. We would not generally consider a wife who shoots her husband for infidelity to be acting morally, but we would recognize the regrettable necessity if she had to use violence to escape from her imprisonment. In the first situation, the wife has the free choice and capacity to *leave* her husband, and thus violence would be an unjust response to the situation; in the second situation, her choice to leave her husband has been eliminated through imprisonment. Infidelity does not destroy a partner's capacity to choose; locking her in the basement does.

AVOIDANCE

If you and I are both standing at the top of a cliff, and I turn to you and say, "Stand in front of me, so I can push you off the cliff," what would your response be? If you do voluntarily stand in front of me, and I then push you off the cliff, this would more likely be considered a form of suicide on your part, rather than murder on my part. The reason for this is that you can very easily *avoid* being pushed off the cliff, simply by refusing to stand in front of me.

Similarly, if I meet you in a bar, and say: "I want you to come back to my place, so I can tie you to the bed and starve you to death," if you do in fact come back to my place, it is with the reasonable knowledge that your longevity will not be enhanced by your decision. On the other hand, if I slip a "date rape" drug into your drink, and you wake up tied to my bed, it is clear that there is little you could have done to avoid the situation.

This question of *avoidance* is key to differentiating aesthetics from ethics. Aesthetics applies to situations that may be unpleasant, but which do not eliminate your capacity to choose.

AVOIDANCE AND INITIATION

There is a particular issue with avoidance that will come up later in this book, which is worth clearing up here beforehand.

If I live on a high mountaintop 5,000 miles away from you, and send you an e-mail telling you that if you ever walk in front of my house, I am going to shoot you, it is relatively easy for you to avoid this situation. My threat of force is certainly immoral, but questions would surely be raised if you immediately jumped on a plane, climbed my mountain and slowly strolled in front of my house.

On the other hand, if you live on a dead-end street, and I tell you that if you take that street to get home, I will shoot you, your capacity to avoid this situation becomes significantly limited. You could certainly tunnel into your house, or jump over a bunch of backyard fences, but all of this would be considerably inconvenient.

In a similar manner, if a representative of organized crime comes to my house and threatens to burn it down if I do not pay regular protection money, I can avoid that specific threat by moving to another continent, but that would seem like a rather unjust way to deal with the situation, since I must now initiate action in order to avoid the threat.

For the moment, we can assume that *any* threat of the initiation of violence is immoral, but the question of avoidance – particularly the *degree* of avoidance required – is also important. In general, the more that a threat interferes with the normal course of daily actions, the more egregious it is. If I have to fly to another continent in order to walk in front of your house, that is scarcely an everyday activity. If I am threatened with violence for walking down the only road towards my own home, that is a far worse intrusion upon my liberties. If I have to take specific and unprecedented action to trigger a threat, that is one thing – if I trigger the threat through normal everyday activities, that is quite another. Telling you I will slap you if you stand on your head on the dark side of the moon is scarcely a threat – telling you I will slap you if you *breathe* is.

ETHICS, AESTHETICS AND AVOIDABILITY

Let's say that you and I agree to meet at a certain location at 6 p.m. sharp – but then I show up half an hour late. What would your reaction be? At first, you may be a little annoyed. If I tell you that I was delayed because I stopped to give a dying man CPR and saved his life, your annoyance would likely be replaced with admiration. On the other hand, if I tell you that I am late because I was playing a video game, your annoyance would probably increase. A dying man's need for CPR is unexpected, and therefore pretty much unavoidable – continuing to play a video game is easily avoidable, and clearly shows a lack of consideration for you.

It is this capacity to *avoid* situations that forms a central root of ethical judgments. A woman raped by a random intruder in her own home is undoubtedly the complete victim of a terrible crime. A woman who gets raped after getting blind drunk at a frat party and dancing naked on a tabletop presents a more complicated case. Clearly the rape, once underway, cannot be avoided, since it is being violently inflicted – however, situations which increase the likelihood of rape can be avoided.

If someone breaks into my house and takes my wallet at gunpoint, I have every right to be outraged. If, however, I leave my wallet sitting on a park bench for a week, do I have the same right to be outraged when I return to find it gone? Instinctively we feel that this would seem to be less justified.

Clearly, this question of avoidance is central to our moral evaluation of cause and effect. Illnesses that strike without warning, and which cannot be prevented, frighten us far more than those that we can avoid. We can minimize the chances of getting lung cancer by refraining from smoking, just as we can help prevent skin cancer by using sunscreen, and avoid broken bones by eschewing extreme sports. Similarly, we can do much to avoid crime through some fairly simple habits, such as choosing moral companions, avoiding locales and situations where crime is more probable, refraining from substance abuse and so on.

There is a phenomenon known as "death by cop," wherein suicidal people provoke an altercation with the police, then pretend to reach for a gun in order to get shot. This is an extreme example of pursuing situations where "victimization" is almost guaranteed. This can also occur in domestic situations, wherein a wife will verbally attack a drunken husband, knowing perfectly well that alcohol inflames his violent temper.

In these situations, we can have some sympathy for the man whose wallet is stolen in the park, or the woman who is attacked at the frat party, or the wife who is beaten by her husband – but at the same time, we would have some significant questions regarding their role or complicity in the wrongs they have suffered. To be just, we must differentiate between a man whose wallet is stolen at gunpoint, and a man who leaves his wallet lying around in a public place. Both men have had their wallets stolen, to be sure, but it would scarcely seem reasonable to hold them equally accountable.

Can the UPB framework help us understand, classify and extend these moral standards?

Initiation

• • •

A REASONABLE MORAL THEORY SHOULD be able to explain all of the above universal standards, just as a reasonable theory of physics should be able to explain how a man can unconsciously calculate the arc of a thrown baseball, and catch it.

If the framework of UPB can explain the above, then it will certainly have passed at least the "common sense" test.

This does not mean that some surprising – even shocking – conclusions may not result from our moral theory, but at least we shall have passed the first hurdle of explaining the obvious, before analyzing that which is far from obvious.

With that in mind, let us turn to the question of *initiation*.

A surgeon can "stab" you with a scalpel, but we can easily understand that his action is very different from a mugger who stabs you with a knife.

This difference can be understood through a further analysis of *initiation*.

If you get cancer, you may ask a surgeon to operate on you. The reason that the surgeon's "stab" is not immoral is that the cancer "initiated" an attack upon your life and health. The surgeon is acting as a "surrogate self-defense agent," just like a man who shoots a mugger who is attacking you. You have also given your consent to the surgeon, and bound his behaviour by a specific contract.

The mugger who stabs you, however, is initiating an attack upon your life and health, which is why his attack is the moral *opposite* of the surgeon's efforts.

If I am a chronic and longtime smoker, I have participated in the chain of events that lead to my lung cancer. By initiating and maintaining the habit of smoking, I have set into motion a chain of causality that can result in a life-threatening affliction. It is certainly possible for me to get lung cancer without smoking – or smoke without getting lung cancer – but I certainly have affected the odds.

Similarly, it is possible for me to leave my wallet on a park bench for a week, return and find it still sitting there, but by leaving it there for such a long time, I certainly have affected the odds of it being gone.

On the other hand, if I stay home every night, I am not exactly courting crime, and so if a maniac invades my home and robs me blind, I cannot be reasonably blamed for any causal role I have played in the incident.

THE NON-AGGRESSION PRINCIPLE (NAP)

A moral rule is often proposed called the *non-aggression principle*, or NAP. It is also called being a "porcupine pacifist," insofar as a porcupine only uses "force" in self-defense. The NAP is basically the proposition that "the initiation of the use of force is morally wrong." Or, to put it more in the terms of our conversation: "The non-initiation of force is universally preferable."

When we analyze a principle such as the NAP, there are really only seven possibilities: three in the negative, three in the positive, and one neutral:

1. The initiation of the use of force is always morally wrong.
2. The initiation of the use of force is sometimes morally wrong.
3. The initiation of the use of force is never morally wrong.
4. The initiation of the use of force has no moral content.
5. The initiation of the use of force is never morally right.

6. The initiation of the use of force is sometimes morally right.
7. The initiation of the use of force is always morally right.

As we have seen above, however, UPB is an "all or nothing" framework. If an action is *universally preferable*, then it cannot be limited by individual, geography, time etc. If it is wrong to murder in Algiers, then it is also wrong to murder in Belgium, the United States, at the North Pole and on the moon. If it is wrong to murder yesterday, then it cannot be right to murder tomorrow. If it is wrong for Bob to murder, then it must also be wrong for Doug to murder.

Uniting the NAP with UPB, thus allows us to whittle these seven statements down to three:

1. It is universally preferable to initiate the use of force.
2. It is universally preferable to *not* initiate the use of force.
3. The initiation of the use of force is not subject to universal preferences.

This is the natural result of applying the requirement of rational consistency to ethical propositions. A rational theory cannot validly propose that opposite results can occur from the same circumstances. A scientific theory cannot argue that one rock must fall down, but another rock must fall up. Einstein did not argue that E=MC^2 on a Thursday, but that E=MC^3 on a Friday, or on Mars, or during a blue moon. The law of conservation – that matter can be neither created nor destroyed – does not hold true only when you really, really want it to, or if you pay a guy to make it so, or when a black cat crosses your path. The laws of physics are not subject to time, geography, opinion or acts of Congress.

This consistency must also be required for systems of ethics, or UPB, and we will subject generally accepted moral theories to this rigour in Part 2, in a few pages.

However, since we are dealing with the question of *consistency*, it is well worth taking the time to deal with our capacity for *inconsistency*.

LIFEBOAT SCENARIOS

• • •

THE FACT THAT UPB ONLY validates logically consistent moral theories does not mean that there can be no conceivable circumstances under which we may choose to act *against* the tenets of such a theory.

For instance, if we accept the universal validity of property rights, smashing a window and jumping into someone's apartment without permission would be a violation of his property rights. However, if we were hanging off a flagpole outside an apartment window, and about to fall to our deaths, few of us would decline to kick in the window and jump to safety for the sake of obeying an abstract principle.

In the real world, it would take a staggeringly callous person to press charges against a man who destroyed a window in order to save his life – just as it would take a staggeringly irresponsible man to refuse to pay restitution for said window. The principle of "avoidability" is central here – a man hanging off a flagpole has little choice about kicking in a window. A man breaking into your house to steal things clearly has the capacity to avoid invading your property – he is not cornered, but is rather the *initiator* of the aggression. This is similar to the difference between the woman whose man cheats on her, versus the woman whose man locks her in the basement.

This is not to say that breaking the window to save your life is not wrong. It is, but it is a wrong that almost all of us would choose to commit rather than die. If I were on the verge of starving to death, I would steal an apple. This does not mean that it is *right* for me to steal the apple – it just means that I would do it – and must justly accept the consequences of my theft. (Of course, if I were such an incompetent or

49

confused human being that I ended up on the verge of starvation, incarceration might be an improvement to my situation.)

GRAY AREAS

The fact that certain "gray areas" exist in the realm of ethics has often been used as a justification for rank relativism. Since on occasion some things remain unclear (e.g. who initiated the use of violence), and since it is impossible to define objective and exact rules for every conceivable situation, the conclusion is often drawn that nothing can *ever* be known for certain, and that no objective rules exist for *any* situation.

This is false.

All reasonable people recognize that biology is a valid science, despite the fact that some animals are born with "one-off" mutations. The fact that a dog can be born with five legs does not mean that "canine" becomes a completely subjective category. The fact that certain species of insects are challenging to differentiate does not mean that there is no difference between a beetle and a whale.

For some perverse reason, intellectuals in particular take great joy in the wanton destruction of ethical, normative and rational standards. This could be because intellectuals have so often been paid by corrupt classes of individuals such as politicians, priests and kings – or it could be that a man often becomes an intellectual in order to create justifications for his own immoral behaviour. Whatever the reason, most modern thinkers have become a species of "anti-thinker," which is very odd. It would be equivalent to there being an enormous class of "biologists" who spent their entire lives arguing that the science of biology was impossible. If the science of biology is impossible, it scarcely makes sense to become a biologist, any more than an atheist should fight tooth and nail to become a priest.

SHADES OF GRAY

In the realm of "gray areas," there are really only three possibilities.

1. There are no such things as gray areas.
2. Certain gray areas do exist.
3. All knowledge is a gray area.

Clearly, option one can be easily discarded. Option three is also fairly easy to discard. The statement "all knowledge is a gray area" is a self-detonating proposition, as we have seen above, in the same way that "all statements are lies" also self-detonates.

Thus we must go with option two, which is that certain gray areas do exist, and we know that they are gray relative to the areas that are not gray. Oxygen exists in space, and also underwater, but not in a form or quantity that human beings can consume. The *degree* of oxygenation is a gray area, i.e. "less versus more"; the question of whether or not human beings can breathe water is surely black and white.

A scientist captured by cannibals may pretend to be a witch-doctor in order to escape – this does not mean that we must dismiss the scientific method as entirely invalid.

Similarly, there can be extreme situations wherein we may choose to commit immoral actions, but such situations do not invalidate the science of morality, any more than occasional mutations invalidate the science of biology. In fact, the science of biology is greatly advanced through the acceptance and examination of mutations – and similarly, the science of ethics is only strengthened through an examination of "lifeboat scenarios," as long as such an examination is not pursued obsessively.

UNIVERSALITY AND EXCEPTIONS

Before we start using our framework of Universally Preferable Behaviour to examine some commonly held ethical beliefs, we must deal with the question of "exceptions."

Using the above "lifeboat scenarios," the conclusion is often drawn that "the good" is simply *that which is "good" for an individual man's life.*

In ethical arguments, if I am asked whether I would steal an apple rather than starve to death – and I say "yes" – the following argument is inevitably made:

1. Everyone would rather steal an apple than starve to death.
2. Thus everyone universally prefers stealing apples to death by starvation.
3. Thus it is *universally preferable* to steal apples rather than starve to death.
4. Thus survival is universally preferable to property rights.
5. Thus what is good for the individual is the ultimate moral standard.

This has been used as the basis for a number of ethical theories and approaches, from Nietzsche to Rand. The preference of each individual for survival is translated into ethical theories that place the survival of the individual at their centre. (Nietzsche's "will to power" and Rand's "that which serves man's life is the good.")

This kind of "biological hedonism" may be a description of the "drive to survive," but it is only correct insofar as it describes what people actually *do*, not what they *should* do.

It also introduces a completely unscientific subjectivism to the question of morality. For instance, if it is morally permissible to steal food when you are starving, how much food can you steal? How hungry do you have to be? Can you steal food that is not nutritious? How nutritious does the food have to be in order to justify stealing it? How long after stealing one meal are you allowed to steal another meal? Are you allowed to steal meals rather than look for work or appeal to charity?

Also, if I can make more money as a hit man than a shopkeeper, should I not pursue violence as a career? It certainly enhances *my* survival... and so on and so on.

As we can see, the introduction of "what is good for man in the abstract – or what most people do – is what is universally preferable" destroys the very concept of morality as a logically consistent theory, and substitutes mere biological drives as justifications for behaviour. It is an explanation of behaviour, not a proposed moral theory.

THE PURPOSE – AND THE DANGERS

With your patient indulgence, one final question needs to be addressed before we plunge into a definition and test how various moral propositions fit into the UPB framework. Since the hardest work lies ahead, we should pause for a moment and remind ourselves why we are putting ourselves through all this rigor and difficulty.

In other words, before we plunge on, it is well worth asking the question: "Why bother?"

Why bother with defining ethical theories? Surely good people don't need them, and bad people don't consult them. People will do what they prefer, and just make up justifications as needed after the fact – why *bother* lecturing people about morality?

Of course, the danger always exists that an immoral person will attack you for his own hedonistic purposes. It could also be the case that, despite clean and healthy living, you may be struck down by cancer before your time – the former does not make the science of morality irrelevant, any more than the latter makes the sciences of medicine, nutrition and exercise irrelevant. One demonstrable effect of a rational science of morality must be to reduce your chances of *suffering* immoral actions such as theft, murder and rape – and it is by this criterion that we shall also judge the moral rules proposed in Part 3 of this book.

The Beast

• • •

AN OBJECTIVE REVIEW OF HUMAN history would seem to point to the grim reality that by far the most dangerous thing in the world is *false ethical systems*.

If we look at an ethical system like communism, which was responsible for the murders of 170 million people, we can clearly see that the real danger to individuals was not random criminals, but *false moral theories*. Similarly, the Spanish Inquisition relied not on thieves and pickpockets, but rather priests and torturers filled with the desire to save the souls of others. Nazism also relied on particular ethical theories regarding the relationship between the individual and the collective, and the moral imperative to serve those in power, as well as theories "proving" the innate virtues of the Aryan race.

Over and over again, throughout human history, we see that the most dangerous instruments in the hands of men are not guns, or bombs, or knives, or poisons, but rather *moral theories*. From the "divine right of kings" to the endlessly legitimized mob rule of modern democracies, from the ancestor worship of certain Oriental cultures to the modern deference to the nation-state as personified by a political leader, to those who pledge their children to the service of particular religious ideologies, it is clear that by far the most dangerous tool that men possess is *morality*. Unlike science, which merely describes what is, and what is to be, moral theories exert a near-bottomless influence over the hearts and minds of men by telling them what *ought* to be.

When our leaders ask for our obedience, it is never to themselves as *individuals*, they claim, but rather to "the good" in the abstract. JFK did not say: "Ask not what

I can do for you, but rather what you can do for me..." Instead, he substituted the words "your country" for himself. Service to "the country" is considered a virtue – although the net beneficiaries of that service are always those who rule citizens by force. In the past (and sometimes even into the present), leaders identified themselves with God, rather than with geography, but the principle remains the same. For Communists, the abstract mechanism that justifies the power of the leaders is *class*; for fascists it is the *nation*; for Nazis it is the *race*; for democrats it is "the will of the people"; for priests it is "the will of God" and so on.

Ruling classes inevitably use ethical theories to justify their power for the simple reason that human beings have an implacable desire to act in accordance to what they believe to be "the good." If service to the Fatherland can be defined as "the good," then such service will inevitably be provided. If obedience to military superiors can be defined as "virtue" and "courage," then such violent slavery will be endlessly praised and performed.

Propaganda

The more false the moral theory is, the earlier that it must be inflicted upon children. We do not see the children of scientifically minded people being sent to "logic school" from the tender age of three or four onwards. We do not see the children of free market advocates being sent to "Capitalism Camp" when they are five years old. We do not see the children of philosophers being sent to a Rational Empiricism Theme Park in order to be indoctrinated into the value of trusting their own senses and using their own minds.

No, wherever ethical theories are corrupt, self-contradictory and destructive, they must be inflicted upon the helpless minds of dependent children. The Jesuits are credited with the proverb: "Give me a child until he is nine and he will be mine for life," but that is only because the Jesuits were teaching superstitious and destructive lies. You could never imagine a modern scientist hungering to imprint his falsehoods on a newborn consciousness. Picture somebody like Richard Dawkins saying the above, just to see how ridiculous it would be.

Any ethicist, then, who focuses on mere criminality, rather than the institutional crimes supported by ethical theories, is missing the picture almost entirely, and serving mankind up to the slaughterhouse. A doctor who, in the middle of a universal and deadly plague, focused his entire efforts on communicating about the possible health consequences of being slightly overweight, would be considered rather deranged, and scarcely a reliable guide in medical matters. If your house is on fire, mulling over the colors you might want to paint your walls might well be considered a sub-optimal prioritization.

Private criminals exist, of course, *but have almost no impact on our lives comparable to those who rule us on the basis of false moral theories.*

Once, when I was 11, another boy stole a few dollars from me. Another time, when I was 26, I left my ATM card in a bank machine, and someone stole a few hundred dollars from my account.

On the other hand, I have had hundreds of thousands of dollars taken from me by force through the moral theory of "taxation is good." I was forced to sit in the grim and brain-destroying mental gulags of public schools for 14 years, based on the moral theory that "state education is a virtue." (Or, rather: "*forced* education is a virtue" – my parents were compelled to pay through taxes, and I was compelled to attend.)

The boy (and the man) who stole my money doubtless used it for some personal pleasure or need. The government that steals my money, on the other hand, uses it to oppress the poor, to fund wars, to pay the rich, to borrow money and so impoverish my children – and to pay the salaries of those who steal from me.

If I were a doctor in the middle of a great city struck down by a terrible plague, and I discovered that that plague was being transmitted through the water pipes, what should my rational response be – if I claimed to truly care about the health of my fellow citizens?

Surely I should cry from the very rooftops that their drinking water was causing the plague. Surely I should take every measure possible to get people to understand the true source of the illness that struck them down.

Surely, in the knowledge of such universal and preventable poisoning, I should not waste my time arguing that the true danger you faced was the tiny possibility that some random individual might decide to poison you at some point in the future.

Thus, as a philosopher concerned with violence and immorality, should I focus on private criminals, or public criminals?

The violations that I experienced at the hands of private criminals fade to insignificance relative to even *one day* under the tender mercies of my "virtuous and good masters."

If, then, the greatest dangers to mankind are false ethical theories, then our highest prioritization should be the discovery, communication and refinement of a valid, rational, empirical and consistent ethical theory. If we discover that most plague victims are dying from impure water, then surely telling them to purify their water should be our first and highest priority.

Let us now turn to that task.

PART 2: APPLICATION

• • •

ETHICAL CATEGORIES

• • •

WITH THE UPB FRAMEWORK IN place, we can now turn to an examination of how UPB validates or invalidates our most common moral propositions. If our "theory of physics" can explain how a man can catch a baseball, we have at least passed the first – and most important – hurdle, and struck our first and deepest blow against the beast.

THE SEVEN CATEGORIES

As mentioned above, propositions regarding universally preferable behaviour fall into three general categories – positive, negative and neutral. To help us separate aesthetics from ethics, let us start by widening these categories to encompass *any* behaviour that can be subjected to an ethical analysis. These seven categories are:

1. It is good (universally preferable and enforceable through violence, such as "don't murder").
2. It is aesthetically positive (universally preferable but not enforceable through violence, such as "politeness" and "being on time").
3. It is personally positive (neither universally preferable nor enforceable, such a predilection for eating ice cream).
4. It is neutral, or has no ethical or aesthetic content, such as running for a bus.
5. It is personally negative (predilection for *not* eating ice cream).
6. It is aesthetically negative ("rudeness" and "being late").
7. It is evil (universally proscribed) ("rape").

Ideally, we should be able to whittle these down to only two categories – universally preferable and aesthetically positive – by defining our ethical propositions so that what is universally banned is simply a mirror image of what is universally preferable, and ditching merely personal preferences and neutral actions as irrelevant to a discussion of ethics.

For instance, the Non-Aggression Principle (NAP) states that the initiation of the use of force is immoral – thus the non-initiation of the use of force is universally preferable, while the initiation of the use of force is universally banned. If what is banned is simply the opposite of what is preferable, there is really no need for an additional category.

Furthermore, as moral philosophers, we must prioritize our examination of rational ethics by focussing on the most egregious violations. Clearly, the most immoral actions must be the violent enforcement of unjust preferences upon others. If actions such as "theft" or "murder" are defined as UPB, the examination of such definitions must be our very highest priority.

Thus we shall focus our efforts primarily on universally preferable and enforceable actions.

VIRTUE AND ITS OPPOSITE

The opposite of "virtue" must be "vice" – the opposite of "good" must be "evil." If I propose the moral rule, "thou shalt not steal," then stealing must be evil, and *not* stealing must be good. This does not mean that "refraining from theft" is the sole definition of moral excellence, of course, since a man may be a murderer, but not a thief. We can think of it as a "necessary but not sufficient" requirement for virtue.

Each morally preferable action must by its very nature have an opposite action – because if it does not, then there is no capacity for choice, no possibility of avoidance, and therefore no capacity for virtue or vice. If I propose the moral rule: "thou shalt defy gravity," then clearly morality becomes impossible, immorality cannot be avoided, and therefore the moral rule must be invalid.

If I propose the moral rule: "thou shalt not go to San Francisco," this can be logically rephrased as: "thou shalt go anywhere but San Francisco." In this way, the moral rule "thou shalt not steal" can be equally proposed in the positive form – "thou shalt respect property rights." Since respecting property rights is a virtue, violating property rights must be a vice.

WHAT IS MISSING

Conspicuously absent from the above list are traditional virtues such as courage, honesty, integrity and so on – as well as their opposites: cowardice, falsehood and corruption.

It may seem that these virtues should fall into the realm of aesthetically positive behaviour, such as being on time, but I for one have far too much respect for the traditional virtues to place them in the same category as social niceties. The reason that they cannot be placed into the category of universally preferable is that, as we mentioned above, the framework of UPB only deals with *behaviours*, not with attitudes, thoughts, states of mind or emotions. The scientific method can process a logical proposition; it cannot process "anger" or "foolhardiness." These states of mind are not unimportant, of course – in fact, they are essential – but they cannot be part of any objective system for evaluating ethical propositions, since they are essentially subjective – and therefore unprovable – states of being.

Thus UPB can only deal with objectively verifiable actions such as murder, assault and so on.

THE FIRST TEST: RAPE

• • •

ALTHOUGH IT IS AN UNPLEASANT topic to discuss, rape is without a doubt the *least* ambiguous action that any moral theory must encompass. Murder can be complicated by self-defense; theft by the problem of starvation or "stealing back" – but one can never rape in self-defense; it is by its very definition the initiation of aggression.

Let us then use the UPB framework to examine the logical consistency of ethical propositions regarding rape, with reference to these seven moral categories.

1. THE GOOD

To take an absurd example, let's imagine that we are reviewing an ethical theory that proclaims that rape is a moral good.

Clearly, if I proclaim that "X" is "the good," then the opposite of "X" must be evil. If *not raping* is good, then *raping* must be evil. Conversely, if *raping* is good, then *not raping* must be evil.

Raping someone is a positive action that must be initiated, executed, and then completed. If "rape" is a moral good, then "not raping" must be a moral evil – thus it is impossible for two men in a single room to *both be moral at the same time*, since only one of them can be a rapist at any given moment – and he can only be a rapist if the other man becomes his victim.

That which enables virtue cannot be evil. "Freedom," for instance, is a prerequisite for virtue – without freedom, we cannot be virtuous – thus "freedom" cannot be evil, since it is *required* for goodness.

If it is morally good to be a rapist, and one can only be a rapist by sexually assaulting a victim, then clearly the victim must be morally good by resisting the sexual assault – since if he does not resist, it is by definition not rape, and therefore not virtuous. In other words, *attacking* virtue by definition *enables* virtue. Thus we have an insurmountable paradox, in which the victim must attack virtue in order to enable virtue – he must resist sexual assault in order to enable the "virtue" of the rapist. Thus not only can the rape victim *not* be virtuous, but he must resist and attack "virtue" in order to allow it.

Insurmountable logical problems thus result from the proposition: "rape is moral." Remember, we agreed that a rational theory cannot propose opposite states for the same situation. All other things being equal, a rock cannot fall both up and down at the same time, and a valid theory cannot predict that one rock will fall up, while another rock will fall down.

In the same way, two men in a room must be considered to be in the same situation. If only one of them can be good, because goodness is defined as rape, and only one of them can rape at any time, then we have a logical contradiction that cannot be resolved.

Also, if we recall that Universally Preferable Behaviour must be independent of time, then we also face a logical problem that, no matter what his physical virility, at some point the rapist will simply be unable to rape anymore, because he will be physically unable to get an erection. At that point, his ability to perform the "good action" becomes impossible. Since "avoidability" is a key criterion for morality, but he is physically unable to be good – in other words, he is unable to avoid being evil – then he cannot be responsible for not raping the other man.

If a man hanging from a tree over a canyon lets go because he lacks the strength to continue holding on, we would not call that a suicide, since the choice to hang on was no longer available to him. If he lets go although he has the strength to continue holding on, the case would not be quite so clear.

THE COMA TEST

Intuitively, it is hard to imagine that any theory ascribing immorality to a man in a coma could be valid. Any ethical theory that posits a positive action as universally preferable behaviour faces the challenge of "the coma test." If I say that giving to charity is a moral absolute, then clearly not giving to charity would be immoral. However, a man in a coma is clearly unable to give to charity, and thus would, by my theory, be classified as immoral. Similarly, a man who is asleep, or has no money to give – or the man currently *receiving* charity – would all be immoral.

This is another central problem with any theory that posits a positive action such as "rape" as moral. At any given time, there are any number of people who are unable to perform such positive actions, who must then be condemned as evil, even though they have no capacity to be "good."

However, if it is impossible to avoid being "evil," then clearly evil as a concept makes no sense. In the example above of the rock crashing down a hill, the rock is not "evil" for hitting your car, since it has no capacity to avoid it of its own free will. If a man's brakes fail right after they have been serviced, then it is not his responsibility for failing to come to a stop. If he has never once had his brakes serviced in ten years, then his irresponsibility is the proximate cause of his continued momentum, and he can be blamed.

In this way, the concept of "avoidability" retains its use. A man in a coma is unable to avoid lying in his bed, since he is in a state of quasi-unconsciousness. Since he is unable to avoid his actions – or inaction in this case – his immobility cannot be immoral.

At this point, the objection can quite reasonably be raised that if a man in a coma cannot be immoral, then he also cannot be moral. However, earlier we said that the opposite of an immoral action must be moral. If we propose the moral rule, "thou shalt not rape," then can we call the man in a coma *moral*, since he does not rape?

CAPACITY

The concept of "avoidability" works in the positive as well as in the negative. If I have lost my genitals in some ghastly accident, am I moral for refraining from rape? It would seem hard to argue that I could be, since genital rape at least is impossible for me. Similarly, we may call a man "generous" if he gives $100 to a beggar – however, we would doubtless revise our estimation if it turned out that he gave away his money while sleepwalking, and woefully regretted his action on waking.

Thus we can reasonably say that where choice is absent, or inapplicable, morality is also absent, or inapplicable. Thus the man in a coma, while his actions cannot be considered evil, neither can they be considered good. He exists in the state without choice, like an infant, or an animal – thus he can be reasonably exempted from moral rules, since there is a physical state that objectively differentiates him from a man who can choose, which is allowable under UPB.

With that in mind, let us continue our examination of rape.

2. AESTHETICALLY POSITIVE

Aesthetically positive actions (APAs) are universally preferable, but not enforceable through violence, since aesthetically negative actions do not initiate the use of force. As we discussed above, if I am late in meeting you, I have not initiated the use of force against you, and I have not removed your capacity to choose, or avoid the situation.

If we say that APAs can be enforced through violence, then we are saying that the initiation of violence is morally good.

If we propose a moral rule that the initiation of violence is morally good, then this rule faces all the same logical impossibilities as the rule that "rape is morally good."

Two men in a room cannot be both morally good at the same time, since one of them must be initiating violence against the other, and the other must be resisting it – since if he is not resisting it, it is by definition not violence, as in the case of the surgeon we discussed above. Thus virtue can only be enabled by resisting virtue, and two men in the same circumstances cannot both be moral at the same time, and so on – all of which are violations of UPB.

Thus we know that rape cannot be an APA.

We can confirm this by reviewing the reasons why "being on time" *is* an APA.

First of all, we instinctively understand that it is more just to reject a friend for being perpetually late than it is to reject a friend for not liking ice cream.

Why is that?

Once again, the UPB framework comes to the rescue.

An APA is *a non-coercive rule that can be rationally applied to both parties simultaneously.*

For instance, if my APA is: "be on time," then it can be a universal standard that can be totally avoided. I cannot forcefully inflict this APA on you because you do not have to be my friend, you do not have to be on time, you do not have to respect or follow my preferences in any way whatsoever. (This is very different from a physical assault, which destroys your capacity for free choice.)

If "being on time" is an APA, then it is possible for two people to achieve it simultaneously – if they are both on time.

With rape though, as we have seen above, it is impossible for two people to perform it at the same time. One must always be the rapist, and the other always the victim.

On the other hand, if I say that "liking jazz" is an APA, then I immediately run into a logical impossibility. Remember, APAs are non-coercive rules that can be rationally applied to both parties simultaneously – the correct formulation for "liking jazz" is: "subjective preferences are universally preferable."

Not only is this a rank contradiction in terms of syntax, but it also immediately fails the test of UPB. If I prefer jazz to all other forms of music, but you prefer classical music to all other forms, and if personal preferences are universally preferable, then you should prefer jazz because I do, and I should prefer classical because you do. This, of course, is impossible, because it would require that we both *simultaneously prefer both jazz and classical above all other forms of music*. You must switch your preference to jazz, because of my preference – but I must at the same time switch my preference to classical, because of your preference. This is like saying that you must both throw and catch the same baseball at exactly the same moment – a logical and physical impossibility.

Since APAs are not enforceable through violence – you cannot shoot a man for being late – then rape *cannot* be an APA, since rape by definition is a sexual attack enforced through violence.

Thus rape cannot fall into the category of APAs.

3. PERSONALLY POSITIVE

Perhaps rape is akin to a merely personal preference. (It cannot be argued that rape does not involve a preference, since rape is a behaviour and, as we have discussed above, all behaviours involve preference.)

The question then arises: can the classification of rape as a merely personal preference stand up to logical scrutiny?

If we propose the moral rule: "personal preferences must be violently inflicted upon other people," how does that stand up to the framework of UPB? (Note that I cannot propose that "personal preferences *may* be violently inflicted upon other people, since that is a violation of UPB, which states that moral rules must be absolute and universal – if they are not, they fall into APA territory, and so cannot be inflicted on others.)

Personal preferences cannot be justly inflicted upon other people, because that would create an insurmountable logical paradox.

If I say that liking the band Queen above all others is universally preferable behaviour, on what grounds could I justify that statement? Only by saying that all personal preferences should be inflicted upon other people. However, if my personal preferences can be inflicted upon you at will, then by the very definition of UPB, your personal preferences can also be inflicted upon *me* at will. Thus we cannot both be moral at the same time, since that would require that we both prefer our own bands while at the same time surrendering that preference to the preferred bands of each other. In other words, I must simultaneously think that Queen is the best band, and that The Police is the best band. This is a logical impossibility, which is a central reason why mere personal preferences cannot be universally enforceable.

Thus if rape is considered to be a merely personal preference, then it cannot logically be enforced upon anybody else. Again, thinking of the two men in a room, this would require that both men prefer to rape each other, but remain utterly unable to enforce that decision, which is not only illogical, but also fortunately completely impractical.

Finally, since personal preferences cannot be enforced on others, but rape is by definition the enforcement of a "preference" upon another, rape cannot be in the moral category of merely personal preferences.

4. Morally Neutral
As discussed above, rape cannot be a morally neutral action, since it is a preference that is enforced upon another.

5. PERSONALLY NEGATIVE

Perhaps rape is a *personally negative* action, the opposite of number three. As an example, a criminal on the run would consider capture a personally negative action (PNA).

Personally negative actions (PNAs) by definition cannot be enforced upon another. Thus a man being raped would be wrong to "inflict" his preference for *not being raped* upon his rapist, in the form of self-defence. In this way, the initiation of violence – the enforcement of a personal preference – is *moral*, while self-defence – also the enforcement of a personal preference – is immoral. Thus we would have the same actions (the enforcement of a personal preference) classified as both moral and immoral, which cannot stand.

6. AESTHETICALLY NEGATIVE

Perhaps rape is an aesthetically *negative* action, like "being late" – the flipside of number two above. However, aesthetically negative actions (ANAs) cannot logically be violently enforced *because by definition they can be avoided*. Since I can freely choose to stop associating with a man who continually shows up late, I cannot shoot him for being late.

However, rape by definition cannot be avoided, since it is a sexual attack enforced through violence. (We can avoid situations which increase the likelihood of rape, but we cannot avoid a rape in progress.) Also, if I choose to stop being friends with the tardy man mentioned above, he cannot justly force me to be his friend by threatening me with violence, since that would rely on the principle that merely personal preferences can be enforced on others, which would run fruitlessly up against my ability to enforce *my* desire to drop his friendship. This kind of "Tarantino morality" always ends up with everyone in a state of mute paralysis, pointing guns at each other's faces like frozen statues.

As we have already established, any universally preferable behaviour must be universal to all people in all places at all times – if ANAs allow for violent enforceability (i.e. I can shoot you for being late) – then if rape is defined as an ANA which can be enforced, then the rape victim who finds rape an aesthetically negative action has the right to shoot his rapist, which effectively affirms the principle of self-defense, but at the expense of also allowing gunplay in the opposition of, say, rudeness.

Thus rape cannot be an ANA.

Which leaves only…

7. EVIL

If rape is defined as evil, then it must involve the *initiation* of the use of force, which clearly it does. Also, the proposition: "rape is evil," passes the "coma test," insofar as it is impossible for a man in a coma to rape someone.

In addition, if rape is evil, then *not* raping must be good – in this way, two men in a room can both be moral at the same time, simply by not raping each other.

Since avoidability is one of the key differentiators between "unpleasant" and "immoral," and rape is clearly an unavoidable behaviour, the definition of "rape as evil" also conforms to this distinction.

Also, since there are times when it is physically impossible to rape someone – for instance, when an erection cannot be attained – the definition of "rape as evil" solves the problem of people being involuntarily immoral, which is by definition impossible, due to the criterion of avoidability.

The rapist may justify his actions by avoiding the proposition "rape is good," and instead substituting another proposition that supports his desire to rape, such as: "It is moral to take one's own pleasure, regardless of the displeasure of others."

This proposition also fails the most basic logical test of UPB. If Bob believes that he should take his own pleasure by raping Doug – regardless of Doug's displeasure – then Bob cannot rationally elevate his preference to a UPB.

If everyone should take their own pleasure regardless of their victim's *dis*pleasure, then Bob has no right to rape Doug, since although Bob *prefers* to rape Doug, Doug most certainly does *not* prefer to be raped. If everyone should take their pleasure regardless of the displeasure of others, then there is no rational reason why Bob's preference to rape Doug should take precedence over Doug's preference to not be raped, regardless of the displeasure that refusing to be raped would cause Bob.

Thus Doug can say to Bob: "It is morally good for me to rape you, because personal preferences can be violently enforced." Bob, of course, can then reply: "It is then morally good for me to violently resist your attack, since my personal preference to not be raped can also be violently enforced."

Of course, few rapists are philosophers, but as we mentioned above, the primary danger to human beings is not the individual criminal, but irrational and exploitive moral theories. For instance, incarceration is inevitably justified through an appeal to a moral theory – and incarceration causes far more people to be raped than private criminals could ever dream of. If the moral theory that justifies incarceration is incorrect, then *correcting* this moral theory should be by far the highest concern of anyone wishing to reduce the prevalence of rape.

Thus it would seem that the only logical possibility for rape is that *not* raping is universally preferable behaviour – or that rape is universally banned behaviour.

Whew!

The fact that the UPB framework has logically and effectively validated the moral proposition that rape is evil – not "good," or "aesthetically preferable," or "personally preferable," or "morally neutral" – is a very good sign. It does not prove beyond a shadow of a doubt that UPB will logically validate all "common sense" moral propositions, but the first hurdle has been passed, and that should give us great cause for celebration. If I were a physicist proposing a Unified Field Theory, and the application of my theory correctly predicted where a thrown baseball would land, I could justly be enormously pleased.

Einstein's theory of relativity predicted that light would bend around a gravity well – when this was first confirmed, it did not prove his theory beyond a shadow of a doubt, but it did prove that the theory *could* be true, which was a great leap forward. The first validation is always the hardest, because it is so easy to get things wrong, and error always outnumbers accuracy.

The UPB framework has correctly validated our moral premise that rape is evil. This is a necessary – but not sufficient – criterion for proof, and fully supports additional investigation.

Thus, let us continue...

The Second Test: Murder

• • •

LET US NOW TEST THE UPB framework against moral propositions regarding *murder*, which here is defined as killing intentionally and with premeditation, not in self-defense.

Since we spent so much time dissecting the question of rape – and since many of the same arguments will apply here – this analysis can be much briefer.

Let us return to our two moral guinea pigs sitting in a room – we'll call them Bob and Doug.

If murder is morally good, then clearly *refraining* from murder is immoral. Thus the only chance that Bob and Doug have to be moral is in the instant that they simultaneously murder each other. Physically, this is impossible of course – if they both stand and grip each other's throats, they will never succumb to strangulation at exactly the same moment. If Bob dies first, his grip on Doug's throat will loosen, thus condemning Doug to the status of *immorality* until such time as he can find another victim. Because Bob dies first – and thus cannot continue to try murdering Doug – Bob's death renders him more immoral than Doug's murder.

Intuitively, we fully recognize the insanity of the moral proposition that murder is good. Logically, we know that the proposition is incorrect because if it is true, it is impossible for two men in a room to both be moral at the same time. Morality, like health, cannot be considered a mere "snapshot," but must be a process, or a continuum. The UPB framework confirms that Bob cannot be "evil" *while* he is strangling Doug, and then achieve the pinnacle of moral virtue the moment that he kills Doug – and then revert immediately back to a state of evil. Moral propositions must be universal, and independent of time and place. The proposition that murder is moral fails this requirement at every level, and so is not valid.

If murder were morally good, then it would also be the case that a man stranded on a desert island would be morally evil for as long as he lived there, since he would have no victims to kill. A man in a coma would also be evil, as would a sleeping man, or a man on the operating table. A torturer would be an evil man as long as he continued to torture – but then would become a good man in the moment that his victim died at his hand.

We can thus see that the proposition that "murder is good" is not only instinctively bizarre, but also logically impossible.

The other objections that applied to the proposition "rape is good" also apply here. Murder cannot be morally neutral, since morally neutral judgments or actions cannot be forcibly inflicted upon another, and murder by definition is forcibly inflicted upon another.

There is also a basic contradiction involved in any universal justification for the act of murder, just as there was in the act of rape. If Bob tries to strangle Doug, but Doug resists, how could Bob rationally justify his actions according to UPB?

Well, he could say something like: "a man's life can be taken any time you want to" – but of course, since UPB is the only valid test of moral propositions, this justifies Doug killing Bob as much as it does Bob killing Doug. Thus Bob can only justify strangling Doug if Doug does not resist in any way – but of course if Doug does not resist, then can it really be considered murder?

Let us say that Bob then adjusts his premise to say: "I can shoot a man in his sleep anytime I want." The problem here is not only the sleep that Bob will lose based on his universal premise, but also the logical impossibility of reversing moral propositions based on the differences in the states of sleeping and waking. Biologically speaking, a man does not become the *opposite* of a man when he falls asleep, any more than gravity reverses when he blinks.

Since a man remains a man when he falls asleep, it cannot be the case that opposite moral rules apply to him in this state. Thus to say that it is immoral to murder a man when he is awake, but it is moral to murder a him when he is asleep, is to create a logical contradiction unsupported by any objective biological facts. A physicist may say that a rock falls down, but a helium balloon rises up – but that is because a rock and a helium balloon have fundamentally different properties. No credible physicist can say that one rock falls down, but that another rock with almost exactly the same qualities falls up. The same is true for moral theories – no credible philosopher can say that morality reverses itself when a man is asleep, since a man's nature does not fundamentally alter when he naps.

In this way, if we cannot justly shoot a man when he is awake, we also cannot shoot him when he is asleep, since he is still a man.

Thus, since the statement "I can shoot a man in his sleep anytime I want" cannot be validated according to UPB, it cannot be a true moral proposition.

Here again we find that the UPB framework holds true in terms of murder. The only possible valid moral theory regarding murder is that it is evil, or universally banned.

We could take the same approach to the question of assault, but the arguments would be identical to those of rape and murder, so for the sake of brevity, we shall continue.

Let us now turn to the question of theft. If this framework holds true here as well, then we have hit the perfect trifecta of our instinctual moral understanding, and found rational confirmation for our existing beliefs. We have discovered the math that explains how we are able to instinctively catch a ball, and that is a necessary start.

SELF-DEFENSE?

We have skirted over the issue of self-defense with regards to murder, though it is scarcely necessary to examine it in the case of rape. This is not because the issue of self-defense is either self-evident or uncomplicated, but rather because the complications that exist can be dealt with more comprehensively after we look at the question of theft.

The Third Test: Theft

• • •

WE WILL HAVE TO SPEND a little bit more time on theft, since it inevitably brings into the picture the question of property rights, which is highly contentious for some.

There are many ways of approaching the question of property rights, from "home-steading" to legal definitions to practical considerations etc. I will address none of those here, because the question of property rights must fall into the framework of UPB, if UPB is to stand as a rational methodology for evaluating moral propositions.

Clearly, the moral proposition with regard to property rights is this: either human beings have the right to own property, or they do not.

Now the first "property" that must be dealt with is the body. "Ownership" must first and foremost consist of control over one's own body, because if that control does not exist, or is not considered valid, then the whole question of morality – let alone property – goes out the window.

UPB is a framework for evaluating moral propositions, or arguments about universally preferable behaviour for all mankind. First and foremost, a man must be responsible for his own actions if they are to be judged morally, since as we have argued above, the capacity to choose actions is fundamental to any ethical evaluation.

If a man has no control over his body, then clearly he has no responsibility for his actions – they are not in fact "his" actions, but rather the actions of his body. Now, no one would rationally argue that if a man strangles another man, it is the murderous fingers that should be put on trial and punished. Clearly, the body cannot entirely control itself, but rather must be to some degree under the direction of the conscious mind.

What this means is that a man is responsible for the actions of his body, and therefore he is responsible for the *effects* of those actions. A man is responsible for where he puts his penis, which is how we know that we can judge him for raping someone. He "owns" the actions of his body as surely as he owns his body. To say that a man is responsible for his body but not the effects of his body is to argue that a man is responsible for aiming and throwing a knife, but not for where it lands.

Also, arguing that a man is not responsible for the effects of his body is a self-detonating statement, similar to the ones we examined above.

If I say to you: "Men are not responsible for the actions of their bodies," it would be eminently fair for you to ask me who is working my vocal chords and mouth. If I say that I have no control over my speech – which is an effect of the body – then I have "sustained" my thesis at the cost of invalidating it completely.

If I am not at all responsible for my speech, then there is no point arguing with me. A tape recorder is also not responsible for its speech, which is why we tend not to get into virulent disagreements with magnetic strips. In cheesy horror movies, young girls seem to be particularly susceptible to demonic possession – the inevitable priest who shows up always offers to talk to the demon in charge of the girl, at which point the girl starts making a sound like Don Ho gargling with ball bearings.

This ridiculous portrait is accurate in one sense though – if some other being is in full control of the girl's vocal chords, it is that being which needs to be addressed, not the girl, who has no control over her responses.

Thus if I say to you that I do not have control over my speech, you can ask me: who does? If I reply that no one does, then it makes about as much sense to argue with me as it does to argue with a television set, or the aforementioned boulder as it bounces down a hillside towards you car.

Thus the very act of controlling my body to produce speech demands the acceptance of my ability to control my speech – an implicit affirmation of my ownership over my own body.

Now, if demonic possession were a valid occurrence, and a girl possessed by a demon spat on a priest, we would not call the *girl* rude, but would rather pity her for being inhabited by such an impolite demon. Whoever has control over the girl's body is culpable for the effects of her actions – this is why we would not call a man who stole while sleepwalking "evil," since he did not have full control over his own body (although we may restrain him in other ways). This is also the basis for the legal defense of "not guilty by reason of insanity," which is that we assume that a man who is insane does not have full control over his actions.

Thus to reject the ownership of the body is to reject all morality, which, as we have seen above, is utterly impossible. Logically, since morality is defined as an enforceable subset of UPB, to reject morality is to say that it is universally preferable to believe that there is no such thing as universal preferences.

Finally, to use one's ownership of one's own body in the form of speech to reject the notion that one can control one's own body, is a blatant and insurmountable self-contradiction.

It is in this way that any rejection of self-ownership can be utterly discarded.

Since we own our bodies, we also inevitably own the *effects* of our actions, be they good or bad. If we own the effects of our actions, then clearly we own that which we produce, whether what we produce is a bow, or a book – or a murder.

PROPERTY AND UPB

Even if we reject the above, we can still use UPB to definitively assert the existence of universal property rights.

As mentioned above, either human beings have property rights, or they do not. Except for a few gray areas, which we will get to shortly, this remains a universal proposition.

If a man does not have the right to use property, then he does not have the right to use his own body. He does not have the right to use his own lungs, and therefore must stop breathing. Although this sounds silly, it is an immediate and inevitable result of the premise that human beings do not have property rights.

It is fairly safe to assume that anyone you are debating property rights with is drawing breath, and thus agrees with you that he has the right to use his own body at least.

The question then comes up whether or not human beings have the right to *exclusive* property use. For instance, property could be defined as a sort of time-share principle of ownership, insofar as everyone should have the right to own everything, on some schedule or another.

This means of course that a man with lung cancer has a right to at least one lung of a healthy person. Since all ownership starts with the body, if we do not have the right to exclusive ownership over our own body, then we must share our body with other people, or be immoral. The sick man has a right to one of our lungs, and if we withhold it from him, that is exactly the same as stealing it. Similarly, both you and I have the right to use Celine Dion's singing voice, since it is wholly selfish of her to pretend that she has exclusive ownership of it.

If human beings do not possess exclusive ownership over their own bodies, then the crime of rape becomes meaningless, since a woman clearly does not exclusively own her vagina, and neither does a man own his own various orifices. If exclusive self-ownership is not an axiom, then even the crime of murder becomes meaningless.

It is no crime to commit suicide, any more than it is to set fire to your own house, since the destruction of one's own property is a valid exercise of ownership. However, if exclusive self-ownership is invalid, then there can be no distinction between murder and suicide. If my liver is failing, and I have a right to take yours, then I can "repossess" it in perfect accordance with morality and honourable behaviour. If this procedure kills you, so what? Without exclusive self-ownership, there is no "you" to begin with...

Thus we can reasonably say that exclusive self-ownership is a basic reality – that all human beings at all times and in all places have exclusive ownership over their own bodies, and thus have exclusive ownership over the effects of their own bodies, both in terms of moral behaviour and property creation or acquisition.

THE GRAY AREAS

Naturally, any statement such as the above brings the inevitable howls of "complexity," which I fully agree with.

Let us say that I mean to give you five dollars as a gift, but by mistake I hand you a $10 bill, saying, "This is for you." Few people would consider it theft if I said, the moment after I handed it to you: "Sorry, I meant to give you five dollars, not ten," and took the larger note back, even though I am taking back property that I have voluntarily relinquished.

On the other extreme, if you are one of my sons, and I pay for your university education, and explicitly tell you that you never need to pay me back, my generosity will doubtless affect your spending habits. It would scarcely seem reasonable for me to clap my forehead after your graduation ceremony and cry, "Oh, I thought you were one of my *other* sons!" and demand repayment.

Similarly, it is generally accepted that children cannot enter into legal contracts, but that adults can. In many societies, the differentiating age is 18 years. This means, of course, that at the stroke of midnight between a man's 17th year and 18th birthday, his capacity to enter into legal contracts arrives fully formed. Has he gone through some massive biological transformation in that split second? Certainly not, although at 18 he is biologically very different than he was at the age of 10, both in terms of physical and mental development.

For the sake of efficiency, if not perfect morality, arbitrary transitions are often placed between one state and another. Childhood is definitely one state; adulthood is quite another. The transition between childhood and adulthood is blended; it is not black and white, but rather like the day descending into dusk, and then night. Noon is definitely not night, and midnight is definitely not daytime, but there are times in between when it is harder to tell, although the direction of the transition is always clear.

In the same way, a man who is greatly mentally deficient can be considered far less responsible for his own actions. A man with an IQ of 65 is mentally scarcely more than a little child – a man with an IQ of 100 is an average adult. If we say that a man with an IQ of 80 becomes responsible, then we are by definition saying that a man with an IQ of 79 is not responsible – is that a clear, fair, and utterly objective demarcation? Certainly not, but in order for most concepts to be practical, the criterion of "good enough" and a reasonable cost/benefit analysis must be put into place. As mentioned above, no water is perfectly pure, but waiting for perfect purity would simply cause a man to die of thirst.

Given that the question of moral responsibility and intellectual capacity only applies to a very small percentage of people right on the border, and that creating objective and perfect tests is very likely to prove impossible, there will inevitably be some "rules of thumb" that win the day. We can only assume that, since biologists live with this kind of occasional subjectivism every day, moral philosophers can somehow survive as well.

Property as Universality

UPB thus gives us clear options with regards to property rights. It cannot be the case that some men have property rights, while other men do not. It cannot be the case that men in Washington have property rights, while women in Baltimore do not. It cannot be the case that men have property rights today, but not tomorrow, and so on.

It also cannot be the case that men have only 50% property rights.

If I argue: "Men only have 50% property rights," then I create yet another insurmountable contradiction. You may well ask me which half of my sentence was *not* generated by me. If I only have 50% property rights, then clearly I only have 50% control over my own body – if I put forward the above sentence, then clearly I am only in control of 50% of that sentence, since I only have 50% control over my voice. Who, then, is responsible for the other 50% of my sentence?

This may sound esoteric, but it is a deadly serious question, for reasons that we will get to shortly.

Let us say that we can somehow magically bypass the "50% ownership of the body" problem, and say that human beings only have 50% property rights when it comes to *external* objects.

How does that work in practice?

Well, if I have two lawnmowers and you have none, then clearly it would be logical for you to have the right to take one of my lawnmowers, since I can only ever own half of my lawnmower collection.

However, when you take possession of one of my lawnmowers, unfortunately you are only ever allowed to own *half* of that lawnmower, since we only have the right to 50% ownership over external objects. Thus you must immediately find somebody with whom you can share the lawnmower. This brings your "just" ownership down to 25%. However, your new co-owner cannot have the right to 25% of the lawnmower, because he only has 50% rights for whatever ownership he possesses – thus he must find somebody to take 50% of the 25% that he has – and so on and so on and so on.

The problem with any theory that argues for less than 100% property rights is that it instantly creates a "domino effect" of infinite regression, wherein everybody ends up with infinitely small ownership rights over pretty much everything, which is clearly impossible.

Thus it must be the case – both logically and practically – that we have full ownership over our own bodies, and over the effects of our bodies, in terms of external property. We do not need a homesteading theory, or other "just acquisition" approaches to justify property rights – they are justified because anybody who acts in any way, shape or form – including arguing – is axiomatically exercising 100% control over his own body, and "homesteading" both oxygen and sound waves in order to make his case.

Thus, by combining this axiomatic reality with UPB, we can easily understand that since anyone debating property rights is exercising 100% control over his own property, the only question is whether or not property rights vary from individual to individual – a question definitively settled by the axiomatic fact of self-ownership, as well as the UPB framework. Any moral proposition must be universal and consistent, and this is how we also know that *everyone* has 100% property rights.

Any other possibility is logically and empirically impossible.

Testing "Theft"

Let us return to our patient moral guinea pigs, Bob and Doug.

If theft is morally good, then once again we face the problem of the impossibility of simultaneous morality. If Bob has a lighter, and it is morally good to steal, then Doug must steal Bob's lighter. However, the moment that Doug is stealing Bob's lighter, Bob cannot himself be moral. The moment *after* Doug steals his lighter, Bob must then steal "his" lighter back – however, it is only "stealing" if the lighter is *not* legitimately Bob's in the first place. When Doug steals Bob's lighter, the lighter does not legitimately become Doug's property, otherwise the concept of theft would make no sense. If, the moment I steal something, it becomes my legitimate property, then restitution would itself become theft. If, however, I do *not* establish legitimate ownership by stealing Bob's lighter, then clearly it is impossible for Bob to "steal" the lighter back, because we cannot steal what we already own, and my theft has not invalidated Bob's ownership of his lighter.

Thus, if stealing is good, then goodness becomes a state achievable only in the instant that Doug steals Bob's lighter. In that instant, only Doug can be moral, and Bob cannot be. After that, goodness becomes impossible to achieve for either party, unless Doug keeps giving Bob's lighter back and then snatching it away again.

Of course, it seems patently ridiculous to imagine that the ideal moral state is for one man to keep giving another man back the property he has stolen, and then immediately stealing it again. Thus logic seems to validate our instinctual understanding of the foolishness of this as a moral ideal – but let's go a little further, to see if it still holds.

Remember, we are not particularly concerned with individual criminals, but rather with moral theories that justify violations of property rights. For instance, if Doug steals Bob's lighter because Doug believes that "No property rights are valid," then Doug's moral theory instantly self-detonates.

If no property rights are valid, then stealing is a completely illogical action, since stealing is an assertion of the just desire to control property.

Property rights themselves are nothing more than the assertion of a just desire to retain control over assets. It is optional, insofar as you and I can join some hippie commune, and decide to never assert our property rights ever again. Or, if it becomes known in my neighbourhood that I am more than happy if somebody takes my property, it seems somewhat more likely that my lawnmower will go missing. Similarly, if I put a notebook computer on my front lawn with a sign saying "yours if you want it," then I am clearly signalling that I have no desire to retain current or future control over the notebook.

If Doug steals Bob's lighter, it is because Doug has a desire to gain control over the lighter – which is the very definition of property rights. If Doug steals Bob's lighter because Doug believes that property rights are invalid, then what he is really saying is: "I want to gain control over Bob's lighter because it is never valid to gain control over any object."

If Doug does steal Bob's lighter, but then defends his theft through a rejection of property rights, then clearly Doug cannot object to Bob taking his lighter *back* – since property rights are invalid, Doug now has no more valid claim to own the lighter than Bob did.

Finally, if Doug steals Bob's lighter under the principle "theft is good," then clearly Doug could have no logical objection to someone else stealing the lighter immediately. However, it would make precious little sense for Doug to spend time and energy stealing Bob's lighter if the moment he had it in his hot little hands, someone else snatched it away from him. In other words, working to gain control of a piece of property is only valid if you can assert your property rights over the stolen object. No man will bother stealing a wallet if he has certain knowledge that it will be stolen from him the moment he gets his hands on it.

In other words, theft in practice is both an affirmation of property rights and a denial of property rights. Any moral theory that supports theft thus both affirms and denies the existence of property rights – an insurmountable contradiction which completely invalidates any such theory.

If we look at the moral aspects of communism, for instance, property rights are explicitly denied for the individual. However, those individuals who call themselves "the government" do claim the right to control property. What this means in practice is that it is *evil* for some men to control property, but it is *good* for other men to control property. Since there is no biological distinction in terms of species between ruler and ruled, we can clearly see that here, for the same species, we have completely opposite moral rules, which cannot be valid. UPB explicitly demands that moral rules be consistent for all men, in all places, and at all times – saying that it is immoral for Ivan Denisovich to exercise his property rights – but *moral* for Joseph Stalin to exercise *his* property rights – creates a rank contradiction, akin to saying that pouring water into a swimming pool both fills it and empties it at the same time. Any physicist who proposed the latter would be laughed out of his profession – moralists, however, regularly propose the former, and are greeted with mysterious levels of respect.

The Fourth Test: Fraud

• • •

RIGHT AT THE EDGE OF what is generally considered ethical sits the challenge of *fraud*.

Fraud is the obtaining of value through false representation. If I tell you that I will ship you an iPod if you give me $200, and then take your money without shipping you the iPod, we instinctively understand that that is a form of theft.

Let us put the problem of fraud through the grinder of UPB, and see whether it holds up.

Clearly, fraud requires that one person *not* be engaged in fraud. In the above potential transaction, if I am hoping to steal your $200, and you are hoping to steal my iPod, nothing will come of it. You will demand the iPod before providing payment, and I will demand payment before providing the iPod. We will be in a stalemate, utterly unable to defraud each other.

Clearly, for fraud to occur, one party must act in good faith. Thus the person who wishes to commit fraud relies on the fact that the other person does *not* wish to commit fraud, in order to prey upon him.

To return to our hapless moral guinea pigs, what would happen if we asked Bob and Doug to act on the moral principle that "fraud is good"?

If Doug has $20, and Bob has a lighter, and Doug offers Bob $20 for that lighter, and then takes the lighter but does not give Bob the $20, then Doug has been acting on the premise that fraud is good.

What happens then?

Clearly, the principle that "fraud is good" cannot be acted on by both Doug and Bob simultaneously – since in order to commit fraud, Doug must act dishonestly, and Bob must act honestly. Thus to enable Doug's "moral" action, Bob must act "immorally."

UPB destroys this possibility, since no valid moral theory can require opposite actions under the same circumstances.

If Doug commits fraud on Bob with the justification that "it is good to lie to get what you want," then clearly it must also be good to be honest as well, since it is impossible to get what you want by lying unless other people are willing to assume your honesty. Thus the premise that it is good to lie to get what you want cannot be achieved unless other people act with integrity – thus lying and honesty are simultaneously required for the fulfillment of the moral principle. This cannot logically stand – that both an action *and its complete opposite* are simultaneously moral in the same place, for the same people, and at the same time.

This is how we know that fraud is wrong.

Again, knowing that fraud is "wrong" simply means that we know that any moral theory that justifies fraud is invalid, because it is self-contradictory. If we build a bridge, and the bridge falls down, we know that the bridge was "wrong" – but the most important thing that we can learn from this disaster is not that the bridge fell down, but to understand the flaws in the theory that caused us to build a bridge that fell down. Similarly, moral theories that cause disasters, such as communism, fascism and Nazism, are important to evaluate relative to UPB not only so we can understand how they went so wrong, but also how to fix our moral theories in the future. Since as a species, we will be forever building bridges, it is essential that we get our facts and theories right, or they will endlessly fall down around us.

However, the question remains whether fraud is evil, or just an aesthetically negative action (ANA).

Fraud is unusual compared to rape, theft and murder, insofar as it requires that the victim act positively to participate in the process. I can jump up behind you and strangle you without any participation on your part, but I cannot defraud you unless you participate to some degree.

Thus fraud falls under the umbrella of "avoidability," and so is in a fundamentally different category than rape, murder and theft. However, the degree of avoidability partly determines the degree of immorality involved. Sending your bank information to a Nigerian email spammer is certainly avoidable; being cheated by an eBay business with a perfect rating is far less avoidable.

There may be certain situations under which fraud is unavoidable, such as "bartering" for a life-saving medicine when no alternative exists, but that falls under the "gray area" that we have discussed above – these occurrences are so rare that they are to ethics as mutations are to biological species.

THE FIFTH TEST: LYING

• • •

THE QUESTION OF *LYING* IS interesting because telling the truth is generally considered to be universally preferable, but not enforceable through violence.

It is generally considered *more* of a strict requirement than "being on time," but *less* strict than "stealing."

What does the UPB framework have to say about this?

Naturally, any moral theory proposing "lying is good" immediately self-detonates, since if the man proposing it *is* lying – which is good – then lying is bad, because he's told the truth that lying is bad.

For instance:

> **Bob**: Lying is always good.
> **Doug**: Are you lying?
> **Bob**: Yes.
> **Doug**: So lying must be bad, since you are lying about it being good.

Or:

> **Bob**: Lying is always good.
> **Doug**: Are you lying?

Bob: No.

Doug: Thus lying is not always good, since you are telling the truth about lying being good.

Lying, however, does not require the initiation of force, and so does not violate the possibility of *avoidability*. Since liars can be avoided, they cannot logically be aggressed against.

Lying also fits more closely in the category of *violence*, insofar as it is moral to lie in self-defense, just as it is moral to use violence in self-defense. It is hard to think of a situation where one would have to "be late" in self-defense, or "be rude." However, if a man bursts into your house and demands to know where your beloved wife is so he can slap her around, it would seem a parody of integrity to refuse to lie to him. Lying in this case would be a form of third-party self-defense, and as morally acceptable as the use of violence in self-defense.

Similarly, if a man obtains a hundred dollars from us by lying, we may justly lie to him to get it back.

Thus we may justly lie to a liar, just as we may justly defend ourselves from a punch with a punch, but we would not exactly respect the escalating pettiness of "repaying" a tardy person by showing up even later.

The difference is that "being late" is not as actively destructive as lying. A tardy person is annoying, but does not fundamentally undermine your capacity to process reality. It's one thing for me to show up an hour late for a 7am meeting – it's quite another to attempt to convince you that we in fact scheduled the meeting for 8am, when I know that this was not the case.

Attacking your confidence in your own mind (sometimes called "gaslighting," after the old movie) is far more egregious than merely making you wait, since it is the act of using another's trust in you to undermine his trust in himself, which is highly corrupt, since it is *using* a value to undermine a value, like counterfeiting.

This is how UPB validates the illogic of the proposition "lying is good," and confirms that the act of lying to someone is worse than "being late," but better than "assault."

More Challenging Tests of UPB

• • •

We have now tested specific moral theories relative to the framework of UPB, and found that UPB validates our most commonly held moral beliefs, such as prohibitions against rape, murder and theft. By bringing the criterion of *avoidability* into our analysis, we have also helped differentiate between crimes that cannot be avoided, and crimes that must be enabled through positive action, such as fraud. Finally, we have divided "preferable behaviour" into three major categories – universal, aesthetic, and neutral (and their relevant opposites). Universally prohibited actions include rape, murder and theft, which force may be used to prevent. Aesthetically preferable actions include politeness, being on time and so on, which cannot be enforced through violence. Neutral actions include purely subjective preferences, or actions that have no moral content, such as running for a bus.

However, there remain many challenging moral tests that fall outside the examples we have dealt with above. We will only deal with a few of those here, to have a look at the framework of UPB, and see how it deals with these more challenging moral questions.

Self-Defense

The concept of self-defense should not be taken for granted. If we assume that there is no such thing as self-defense, or that self-defense is never a valid action, then the framework of UPB undoes that assumption very quickly.

If there is no such thing as self-defense, then we are not talking about the initiation or the retaliation of the use of force, but rather just the use of force in any context.

In other words, if we get rid of the concept of self-defense, the only question that we need to ask ourselves is: *is it universally preferable to use force, or not?*

If it were universally preferable to use force, then no human being should ever advance a moral argument, but should rather use force to achieve his ends. However, just as in the rape, theft and murder examples cited above, the claim that it is universally preferable to use force immediately invalidates itself. To be able to use force upon another person requires that that person submit to force – in other words, in order for one person to be moral, the other person must be immoral, which cannot stand. Also, if the other person *submits* to force, it is not force – thus he must *resist*, which requires that he resist virtue in order to enable virtue, which is self-contradictory.

In addition, if it is always preferable to use force, then crimes such as rape and murder become irrelevant, because if it is always preferable to use force, then love-making becomes immoral, and rape becomes moral – but only for the rapist, while *submission* to violence, rather than violence itself, becomes moral for his victim, which is a contradiction.

If, on the other hand, we say that violence is bad, then we open up the possibility of self-defense. If it is a UPB-compliant statement to say that violence is evil, then we know that, since that which is evil can be prevented through the use of violence, the use of violence to *oppose* violence is morally valid.

Thus, since we know that violence is evil, we know that we may use force to oppose it. If we define an action as evil, but also prevent anybody from acting against it, then we are no longer moral philosophers, but merely judgemental archeologists. This would be akin to a medical theory that said that illness is bad, but that it is evil to attempt to prevent or cure it – which would make no sense whatsoever.

Also, if human beings cannot validly act to prevent harm to themselves, then actions such as inoculations, wearing gloves in the cold, putting on sunscreen or insect repellent, building a wall to prevent a landslide, brushing one's teeth, wearing shoes and so on are all immoral actions.

If we return to Bob and Doug, and we give them the moral argument that self-defense is always wrong, what results?

Well, we create another paradox. Self-defense is the use of violence to prevent violence. If self-defense is always wrong, then it cannot be violently "inflicted" upon an attacker. However, preferences that cannot be inflicted upon others fall into the APA or morally neutral category. To place the violence of self-defense into these categories is to say that violence cannot be inflicted on others – but the very nature of violence is that it *is* inflicted on others, and thus this approach results in a surfeit of contradictions.

Self-defense cannot be "evil," since evil by definition can be prevented through force. However, self-defense is a response to the initiation of force, and thus cannot be prevented through force, any more than you can stop the motion of a soccer ball by kicking it violently.

Self-defense also cannot be *required* behaviour, since required behaviour ("don't rape") can be enforced through violence, which would mean that anyone failing to violently defend himself could be legitimately aggressed against. However, someone failing to defend himself is *already* being aggressed against, and so we end up in a circular situation where everyone can legitimately act violently against a person who is not defending himself, which is not only illogical, but morally abhorrent.

If Bob attacks Doug, but it is completely wrong for Doug to use violence to defend himself, then violence ends up being placed into two moral categories – the initiation of force is morally good, but self-defense is morally evil, which cannot stand according to UPB.

However, you might argue, does not the proposition that self-defense is good also make violence both good and bad at the same time – the violence that is used to attack is bad, but the violence that is used for self-defense is good?

This is an interesting objection – however, if the initiation of force is evil, then it can be prohibited by using force, since that is one of the very definitions of evil that we worked out above.

Thus it is impossible for any logical moral theory to reject the moral validity of self-defense.

Child Raising

Instinctively, we generally understand that there is something quite wrong with parents who do not feed their babies. To conceive a child, carry a child to term, give birth to the child, and then leave it lying in its crib to starve to death, severely offends our sensibilities.

Of course, our offence is in no way a moral argument, but it is an excellent starting place to test a moral theory.

Before, when we were talking about UPB, we noted that, where there are exceptions in UPB, there must be objective differences in biology. Or, to put it more accurately, where there are objective differences in biology, there may be rational exceptions or differences in UPB. A child of five has a biologically immature brain and nervous system, and thus cannot rationally process the long-term consequences of his actions. It is the immature brain that is the key here, insofar as if an adult male is retarded to the point where his brain is the equivalent to that of a five year old, he would also have a reduced responsibility for his actions.

Thus when we point to situations of reduced responsibility, we are not taking away responsibility that exists, but rather recognizing a situation where responsibility does not exist, at least to some degree. If I say that a man in a wheelchair cannot take the escalator, I am not *taking away* his right to take the escalator, but merely pointing out that he cannot, in fact, use it. When I say that UPB does not apply to the actions of a five year old, I am not saying that UPB is subjective, any more than a height requirement for a roller coaster somehow makes the concept of "tall" subjective.

If I voluntarily enter into a contract with you wherein I promise to pay your bills for a year, I have not signed myself into slavery, but I certainly have taken on a positive obligation that I am now responsible for.

If I run a nursing home, and I take in patients who are unable to feed themselves, then if I do not feed those patients, I am responsible for their resulting deaths. No one is *forcing* me to take in these patients, but once I have expressed a desire and a willingness to take care of them, then I am responsible for their continued well-being.

In the same way, if I borrow your lawnmower, I am obligated to bring it back in more or less the same state that it was when I borrowed it. Similarly, if I go to a pet store and buy a dog, I have taken on a voluntary obligation to take care of that dog. This does not mean that I am now the dog's slave until the day it dies, but it does mean that as long as the dog is in my possession, I have a responsibility to try to keep it healthy.

These kinds of implicit contracts are quite common in life. We do not sign a contract with a restaurateur when we go to eat a meal in his restaurant; it is simply understood that we will pay before we leave. I have never signed a contract when I walk into a store promising not to shoplift, but they have the right to prosecute me if I do. I also have never signed a contract promising not to rape a woman if we go on a date, yet such a "contract" certainly exists, according to UPB.

If I run a nursing home, and disabled people rely on me to feed them, if I prove unable to feed them for some reason, then my responsibility is clearly to find somebody else who will feed them. The grave danger is not that *I* don't feed them, but rather that everyone else thinks that I *am* feeding them, and so do not provide them food. This accords with an old moral argument about diving into a river to save someone from drowning. I am not obligated to dive into a river to save someone from drowning, but the moment that I do – or state my intention openly – then I am responsible for trying to save that person, for the very practical reason that everyone else thinks that I am going to save that person, and so may not take direct action themselves.

Thus it is assumed that parents will feed and take care of their newborn baby. If said parents decide against such care-giving, then they are obligated to give the child up to other people who *will* care for it, or face the charge of murder, just as the manager of a home for the disabled must either feed those who utterly depend on him, or give them up to someone who will. If I decide that I no longer want to take care of my dog, I must find him another home, not simply let him starve to death.

This all relies on the principle of third-party self-defense, which is fully supported by the framework of UPB, since the right of self-defense is universal. If I see a man in a wheelchair being attacked by a woman, I have the right to defend him – and this is all the more true if he lacks the capacity to defend himself.

Since children cannot feed themselves, earn a living or live independently, they are the moral equivalent of kidnap victims, or the wife we talked about before whose husband locked her in the basement. Children also lack the capacity for effective self-defense, due to their small stature and near-complete dependence upon their parents.

Thus since it is certainly the case that we have the right to act in self-defense for someone else – and that right becomes even stronger if that person cannot act in his own self-defense, it is perfectly valid to use force against parents who do not feed their children, just as it is perfectly valid to use force against the husband who is starving his wife to death by locking her in the basement.

As we also mentioned above, the less able a victim is to avoid the situation, the worse the crime is. Even the wife who ends up locked in the basement has at least *some* ownership in the matter, because she chose to marry this evil lunatic to begin with. Once she is locked in the basement, the situation is unavoidable, yet there were doubtless many clues hinting at her husband's abusive nature, from the day she first met him.

Children, however, are the ultimate victims, because they never had any chance to avoid the situations they find themselves in.

Thus we can logically establish the responsibility of parents towards their children by using the UPB framework. Since every person is responsible for the effects of his or her body, and children are an effect of the body, then parents are responsible for their children. Since everyone has the right to self-defense, for themselves and for others – since it is a universal right – then anyone can act to defend children. Since everyone must fulfill voluntary obligations, and having children is a voluntary obligation, parents must fulfill those obligations related to children. Since, through inaction, causing the death of someone completely dependent upon you is the equivalent of murder, parents are liable for such a crime.

We could of course put forward the proposition that parents do not have to take care of their children, but that is far too specific a principle to be a moral premise – it would be the same as saying "parents can murder," which is not UPB-compliant, and so would require a biological differentiation to support an exception – and becoming a parent does not utterly overturn and reverse one's biological nature.

Parents who starve a child to death are clearly guilty of murder. Children are born into this world in a state of involuntary imprisonment within the family – this does not mean that the family is evil, or corrupt – it is simply a statement of biological fact. Children are by the parents' choice enslaved to the parents – this form of biological incarceration puts negligent parents in the same moral position as a kidnapper who allows his captive to starve to death, or a nurse who lets her utterly-dependent patients die of thirst.

"DON'T EAT FISH"
What would be the status of the moral proposition: "It is evil to eat fish"?

Clearly, this proposition seems to satisfy at least some of the requirements of UPB – it appears universal, independent of time and place, and relatively objective.

Yet it seems hard for us to reasonably call this a truly *moral* theory – why?

First of all, "evil" encompasses actions that can be prevented through the use of force. Rape is "evil," and so I can use force to defend myself against someone attempting to rape me.

Can I justly shoot someone who eats a piece of fish?

It would seem silly to argue that I can – but why?

There are some objective limits to the universality of this doctrine. For instance, some people may have no access to fish – they may live in a desert, say – while others live by a lake teeming with fish, and find it hard or impossible to survive without eating them. However, that can't be quite enough, since we have already accepted the fact that the inability of a eunuch to rape does not invalidate the moral proposition "it is evil to rape."

No, the "red herring" in the moral proposition "It is evil to eat fish" is the word *"fish."*

A scientist cannot validly say that his theory of gravity only applies to pink rocks. Since his theory involves gravity, it must apply to *all* entities that have mass.

Similarly, in the example above, UPB accepts only the *act* of eating, and rejects *what* is being eaten, since what is being eaten is not an *action*, but rather what is being acted upon.

In the same way, an ethicist cannot validly put forward the moral proposition: "It is evil to rape the *elderly*." "Rape" is the behaviour; whether the victim is elderly or not is irrelevant to the moral proposition, since as long as the victim is human, the requirement for universality remains constant. "Thou shalt not steal" is a valid moral proposition according to UPB – "thou shalt not steal *turnips*" is not, for the simple reason that theft is related to the concept of property – and turnips, as a subset of property, cannot be rationally delineated from all other forms of property and assigned their own moral rule.

The moral proposition "eating fish is evil" thus fails the test of universality because it is too specific to be generalized – it is like saying "my theory of gravity applies only to pink rocks." If it is a theory of gravity, then it must apply to everything; if it only applies to pink rocks, then it is not a theory of gravity.

UPB also rejects as invalid any theory that results in opposing moral judgments for identical actions. "Assault" cannot be moral one day, and immoral the next. Thus we know that "eating" cannot be moral one day, and immoral the next.

Either "eating" is moral, immoral, or morally neutral. If eating is immoral, then a whole host of logical problems arise, which I am sure we are quite familiar with by now.

If, on the other hand, eating is *moral*, then it cannot be moral to eat a cabbage, and immoral to eat a fish, since that is a violation of universality, insofar as the same action – eating – is judged both good and bad.

It is in this way that we understand that the proposition "eating fish is evil" fails the test of UPB, and is not valid as a moral theory.

ANIMAL RIGHTS

We do not have the time here to go into a full discussion of the question of animal rights, but we can at least deal with the moral proposition: "it is evil to kill fish."

If it is evil to kill fish, then UPB says that anyone or anything that kills the fish is evil. This would include not just fishermen, but sharks as well – since if killing *fish* is evil, we have expanded our definition of ethical "actors" to include non-human life.

It is clear that sharks do not have the capacity to refrain from killing fish, since they are basically eating machines with fins.

Thus we end up with the logical problem of "inevitable evil." If it is evil to kill fish, but sharks cannot avoid killing fish, then sharks are "inevitably evil." However, as we have discussed above, where there is no choice – where *avoidability* is impossible – there can be no morality. Thus the proposition "it is evil to kill fish" attempts to define a universal morality that includes non-moral situations, which cannot stand logically.

Also, the word "fish" remains problematic in the formulation, since it is too specific to be universal. The proper UPB reformulation is: "it is evil for people to kill living organisms."

If, however, it is evil to kill, we again face the problem of "inevitable evil." No human being can exist without killing other organisms such as viruses, plants, or perhaps animals. Thus "human life" is defined as "evil." But if human life is defined as evil, then it cannot *be* evil, since avoidance becomes impossible.

What if we say: "it is evil to kill people" – would that make a man-eating shark evil?

No – once again, since sharks have no capacity to avoid killing people, they cannot be held responsible for such actions, any more than a landslide can be taken to court if it kills a man.

UPB allows for exceptions based on objective and universal material or biological differences, just as other sciences do. The scientific theory that gases expand when heated applies, of course, only to gases. I cannot invalidate the theory by proving that it does not apply to, say, plastic.

In the same way, morality only applies to rational consciousness, due to the require-ment for avoidability. If I attempt to apply a moral theory to a snail, a tree, a rock, or the concept "numbers," I am attempting to equate rational consciousness with entities that may be neither rational nor conscious, which is a logical contradic-tion. I might as well say that the Opposite Angle Theorem in geometry is invalid because it does not apply to a circle, or a cloud. The OAT only applies to intersect-ing lines – attempting to apply it to other situations is the conceptual equivalent of attempting to paint air.

In other words, misapplication is not disproof.

There are many other "gray areas" that we could work on, from abortion to intel-lectual property rights to restitution and so on, but I think that it is far more important to take UPB out of the realm of abstraction, and begin applying it to the real world problems we face today.

Part 3: Practice

• • •

The Value of Universally Preferable Behaviour

• • •

A NEW THEORY IS OF precious little value if it only points out the obvious. If physics only provided an accurate description of how we catch a ball, then physics would not be a very worthwhile pursuit, because we already *can* catch a ball. Discovering that the world is round only aids in long-distance navigation across the sea – it does nothing to help us get downtown. Quantum mechanics only becomes useful when other methodologies cannot provide the necessary accuracy – it does not help in building a car.

In the same way, the UPB framework, and the moral rules that it validates or rejects, should ideally provide us with some startling insights about the world that we live in, and our relations to each other.

If all that UPB did was to prove that rape, murder and theft are morally wrong, it would not add much value, since almost no one believes that those things are morally right to begin with.

Thus let us begin applying this framework to the world that we live in, and see what value comes out of it.

THE "NULL ZONE" REVISITED

• • •

AT THE BEGINNING OF THIS book, I put forward a way of looking at how we process truth, analogizing it to physics. From the "little truths" of catching a baseball, we arrive at the "great truths" of physics – and the great truths cannot contradict the little truths.

The same is true of morality. From the little truths of "I should not murder" we can get to the great truths such as "the initiation of the use of force is morally wrong."

In the realm of physics, a central barrier to the logical extrapolation of truths from personal experience to universal theory has been religion.

For instance, no man has ever directly experienced a perfect circle – such an entity exists in the abstract, and in mathematics, but neither can be visualized in the mind, nor sensually experienced in the real world. Nowhere in nature, to our knowledge, does a perfect circle exist, either in the "little truths" of personal experience, or the "great truths" of physics.

However, for thousands of years, the science of astronomy was crippled by the quest for this "perfect circle." Planetary orbits had to be perfect circles, because God would never allow anything as "imperfect" as an ellipse in His creation.

The problem with this approach – well, one problem anyway – was the retrograde motion of Mars. From our planet, Mars at times appears to be moving "backwards," as Earth "overtakes" it around the sun. The false belief that the Earth was the centre of the solar system, combined with a mania for "perfect" circles, produced the Ptolemaic system of astronomy, which multiplied all of these perfect circles to the point of absurdity, in order to take into account elliptical orbits and the retrograde motion of Mars.

Why was this illusion of perfection considered to be a requirement for celestial bodies? Certainly the evidence of the moon, with its pitted and cratered surface, would seem to support the imperfection of the heavens, but religious fixations bypassed the direct sensual evidence of both immediate and interplanetary imperfections. Galileo's discoveries of moon-mountains, sunspots and Jupiter's moons were all attacked as heretical.

We can also turn this analysis to the question of the existence of God as well.

We have no direct, empirical or rational evidence for the existence of God. The most abstract scientific measurements provide no evidence for the existence of God either – yet in between the truth of our own experience, which is that there is no God, and the most abstract scientific measurements and theories – which also confirm that there is no God – a sort of "null zone" is willed into existence, *which completely inverts any rational standards of truth.*

BIGOTRY

Beliefs may be true, false, or *anti-truth*. It is a true belief that the Sahara Desert is in North Africa; it is a false belief that the Sahara is in Scotland; it is an *anti-true* belief that the Sahara is whatever I want it to be, and exists wherever I want it to exist. The first belief is true; the second is false – the third is a bigoted assertion that detonates the very concept of proof.

We can say:

1. Proposition X is true because it is rational.
2. Proposition Y is false because it is irrational.
3. Proposition Z is true because I *want* it to be true.

The third assertion is a complete self-contradiction. "Truth" is independent of desire, since desire is by definition a subjective preference, and truth is by definition the conformity of ideas to the objective standards of logic and empirical reality. Saying that something is true because you *want* it to be true is to equate subjectivity with objectivity, which is a self-contradictory statement.

Bigoted assertions – or "faith" – by definition cannot be tested, since they are not belief in the *absence* of evidence, but belief in *defiance* of reason and/or evidence.

We can believe unproven things that turn out to be true – someone doubtless thought that the world was round before it was proven – but the "null zone" is the realm wherein we cling to a belief in things that *could not possibly turn out to be true.*

If I say that two plus two equals five, I am making a mistake that can be corrected with reference to logic. If I say that I believe that a square circle exists, then I am making an explicitly self-contradictory statement, which disproves itself. If I go further, however, and emphatically claim that "foo plus tury equals desty" – and refuse to define any of my terms – I am making a statement to which logic and evidence *cannot be applied.*

Next Stop: the "Alternate Universe"

In general, the way that people try to "save" their anti-empirical and anti-logical beliefs is to create an "alternate realm" or "alternate universe" wherein their self-contradictory statements can somehow be true.

If I say: "A square circle exists," I am asserting that which is clearly impossible within this universe. Thus, if I wish to retain my belief, I must invent some *other* universe, or realm "outside" this universe where a square circle can exist.

If I make up a realm where self-contradiction equals truth, I can then claim that those who say that a square circle does *not* exist are themselves bigoted and prejudicial, because they are eliminating possibilities that *could* be true. (This inevitably ends up with comparisons to those who said that Einsteinian physics was impossible, that the world could not be round and so on. Uncertainty in *content* – i.e. theory – is somehow supposed to be equated with uncertainty in *methodology*, i.e. reason and evidence. The fact that a mathematical theorem can be disproved does not disprove the principles of mathematics, but rather confirms them.)

With regards to this "null zone," only two possibilities really exist. Either this *null zone* exists completely independently of our universe, and will never be measurable, detectable or discoverable in any way, shape or form – or, at some point, we shall be able to detect and interact with this magical land where self-contradiction equals truth.

If, at some point, it turns out that we *are* able to interact with this *null zone*, then we shall have direct sensual or rational evidence of its existence. In other words, it must "protrude" into our universe in some manner. However, the moment that it becomes detectable in our universe, it must have rational and empirical existence, like everything else we can detect. Thus these otherworldly "protrusions" into our universe *cannot create the capacity for our universe to support the existence of a square circle.*

We can thus be certain that if we *are* ever able to detect this other universe, the evidence we gather will in no way support the existence of self-contradictory statements. Square circles, gods and other self-contradictory concepts cannot hide there, any more than they can hide in the wet dreams of leprechauns.

On the other hand, if it turns out that we are *never* able to detect this other universe, and it remains a completely theoretical entity, with no evidence or rationality to support it, then it is simply a conceptual bag in which it is "convenient" to place things that are obviously not true.

EXISTENCE VERSUS NON-EXISTENCE

• • •

WE DEFINE "NON-EXISTENCE" AS THAT which does not possess mass or energy, or display the effects of mass or energy, such as detectable relationships like gravity.

God does not possess mass or energy, or display the effects of mass or energy – God in fact is not detectable or verifiable in any way, shape or form, either through the senses, or through rationality.

Thus if I say, "God exists," what I am really saying is:

"That which exists must be detectable; God cannot be detectable, but God exists – therefore that which does not exist, exists."

In other words, by saying "God exists," I have created an insurmountable contradiction. I have defined "existence" as "non-existence," which makes about as much sense as defining "life" as "inanimate matter," or a rock as "the opposite of a rock," or a "square" as a "circle."

Similarly, if I create some alternate universe where "non-existence equals existence" and "contradiction equals consistency" and "truth equals falsehood" and "irrationality equals rationality," then what I have really done is create a realm called "error," put everything in it which is not true, and defined this realm as a place where "error equals truth."

(Let's not even get *started* on the logical nightmare of the truth value contained in the statement "error equals truth.")

Of course, people do not create this "alternate universe" in order to invalidate truth within our own universe, but rather to rescue that which is erroneous in reality, and call it true. For instance, no one who argues "God may exist in another universe, so you cannot claim that God does not exist" ever argues "*I* may not exist in that other universe, so you cannot claim that I exist here."

They also tend not to respond well to the argument that: "In another universe, you may be agreeing with me that God does not exist, so that makes you an atheist." (This argument tends also not to work very well with math teachers – I have never seen a student successfully argue that an incorrect answer may be correct in another universe, and so it is unjust to mark it as wrong.)

If valid statements about reality can be endlessly opposed because some imaginary realm called "error equals truth" invalidates them, then what is really being said is "no positive statements about truth can be valid" – however, we are wise enough as philosophers by now to know that this very statement is self-contradictory, since it is a positive statement considered to be true that says that no positive statements can be true.

If nothing can be true or false – even that statement – then no statements whatsoever can be made about anything. Using words, using English, using comprehensible sentences – all make no sense whatsoever, since in this "alternative universe" such structured utterances may be complete nonsense. If things which can be true in this alternate universe have an effect on statements we make in this universe, then clearly the reverse is also true, which means that no statements can ever be made about anything, since their exact opposite can be equally true.

The true reality of the statement "error equals truth" is the tautological insanity of "null equals null."

THE "ALTERNATE UNIVERSE" IN HUMAN SOCIETY

The reason that we have been spending so much time dealing with this "alternate universe" theory is that it has direct relevance to human society, and is used to "justify" the greatest evils which are committed among us.

In our own personal experience, we know that murder is wrong. In working through the proposition that murder is morally wrong in the above examples, I strongly doubt that anyone was shocked to have their moral instincts confirmed through the strict abstract reasoning of UPB.

In this section, however, it is officially permissible for you to begin to be truly shocked.

The greatest leaps forward in scientific understanding are the so-called "unifying theories." Einstein spent decades trying to work out a unified field theory; and theories of physics which unite strong and weak forces, electromagnetism, gravity and so on remain elusive.

UPB as a framework, however, not only justifies our moral instincts at the personal, philosophical and universal levels – but also has profound and shocking implications for human society.

UPB In Action

The UPB framework validates moral propositions by demanding that they be internally consistent, and universal in terms of time, place and individuals.

If we accept UPB, we must also accept the following corollary:

* Moral propositions are independent of costume.

What this means is that a man cannot change his moral nature along with his clothing. The act of changing one's costume does not alter one's fundamental nature. Thus opposing moral rules cannot be valid based on the clothes one is wearing.

Soldiers, of course, wear costumes that are different from the average citizen. The average citizen is forbidden to murder; soldiers, however, are not only *allowed* to murder, but are morally *praised* for murdering.

Let's take another example.

Theft is morally wrong, as we have seen above. It is morally wrong for all people in all situations at all times and under all circumstances.

Since theft is the forcible removal of somebody else's property without consent, then taxation is always, universally and forever a moral evil. Taxation is by definition the forcible removal of somebody's property without their consent, since taxation relies on the initiation of the use of force to strip a man of his property.

What we call "the government" is merely another example of this *null zone* wherein up is down, black is white, truth is falsehood and evil is good.

Society progresses exactly to the degree that reason and evidence make the great leap from the personal to the universal, and destroy any irrational *null zones* in the way. Science progresses exactly to the degree that it rejects the irrationality of God and subjective "absolutes." Medicine progresses exactly to the degree that it rejects the efficacy of prayer and empty ritual, and instead relies on reason and evidence.

Philosophy also – and human society in general – will advance exactly to the degree that it rejects the irrational "square-circle morality" of statist and religious ethical theories.

Government

Saying that the government operates under opposite moral rules from the rest of society is exactly the same as saying, "leprechauns are immune to gravity." First of all, leprechauns do not exist – and one of the ways in which we know that they do not exist is that it is claimed that they are immune to gravity. Everything that has mass is subject to gravity – that which is immune to gravity by definition does not have mass, and therefore does not exist. The statement "leprechauns are immune to gravity" is a tautology, which only confirms the nonexistence of leprechauns – it is the semantic equivalent of "that which does not exist, does not exist." A is A, Aristotle's first law of logic, does precious little to confirm the existence of that which is defined as non-existence.

In the same way, when we say that it is morally good for soldiers to murder and government representatives to steal, we know that "soldiers" and "government representatives" as moral categories are *completely invalid.*

If I say that a square circle has the right to steal, I am merely saying that that which cannot exist has the right to do that which is self-contradictory – a purely nonsensical statement, but one which remains strangely compelling in the "null zone" of politics.

If I buy a soldier's costume at a second hand store, and put it on, clearly I have not created an alternative universe wherein opposite moral rules can be valid. The moment before I put the costume on, it was wrong for me to murder – when does it become *right* for me to murder? When I put on the trousers? What if I have the trousers on, but not the vest? What if I have only one boot on? What about if both boots are on, but only one is laced? What if my hat is on backwards? What if I have put on a uniform that is not recognized by the first person I come across? Did the Beatles suddenly possess the right to murder when they shot the cover for "Sergeant Peppers"? Did they lose that right when they took off their jackets?

I ask these rhetorical questions because they are in fact deadly serious. Clearly, a military costume does not change the nature of a human being, any more than a haircut turns him into a duck, a concept, or a god.

"Ah," you may say, "but the costume is invalid because you got it at a second hand store – putting on the uniform of the soldier no more makes you a soldier than photocopying a doctorate gives you a Ph.D."

The analogy is incorrect, because having a Ph.D. or photocopying a doctorate does not change any of the moral rules that you are subjected to as a human being.

"Well," you may reply, "but the difference is that the soldier possesses moral rights that are provided to him by the average citizen, for the sake of collective self-defense and so on."

This raises a very interesting point, which is the question of whether opinions can change reality.

OPINIONS AND REALITY

Clearly, we understand that I cannot through my opinion release you from the restraints of gravity, any more than my opinion that "2+2=5" makes it true.

"Opinions" are those beliefs which have no clear evidence in reality, or for which no clear evidence can be provided, or which are expressions of merely personal preferences. My personal opinion is that I prefer chocolate ice cream to vanilla – I may also have an "opinion" that Iceland is a tropical paradise, or that God exists, or that rain falls upward. Personal opinions clearly have nothing to do with morality; opinions that claim to accurately describe reality, but which do not, are merely incorrect prejudices. Believing that the rain falls upward does not reverse its course; wearing a Hawaiian shirt to Iceland does not make Reykjavik any warmer.

Thus believing that murder is morally good does not make murder morally good. Since my beliefs about a human being do not change his moral nature, my belief that his murders are virtuous does not change the virtue of his actions. If I close my eyes and imagine that you are a lizard, you do not suddenly lose your ability to regulate your own body temperature. Imagining that you are a fish does not bypass your need for scuba gear.

Opinions do not change reality.

Because opinions do not change reality, I cannot grant you any exception or reversal with regards to a universal moral rule. Since moral rules are based on universal logic, as well as the physical nature and reality of a human being, I cannot grant you the "right to murder," any more than I can grant you the ability to levitate, walk on water or accurately say that two and two make five.

GOVERNMENT AS VOLUNTARISM

The open force involved in the institution of government – the conceptual wrapper that reverses moral rules for a particular group of individuals – is something that is always kept off the table in debates. When talking about government, it is never considered a positive thing to point out "the gun in the room." Almost by definition, governments are considered to be chosen by and for the people, and to operate with their expressed or implicit approval.

However, this is pure nonsense.

If a man holds a knife to a woman's throat while having sex with her, that is by any definition an act of rape. He cannot say that the sex is consensual, while at the same time threatening her with injury or death if she refuses to have sex with him. If the sex is voluntary, then the knife is completely unnecessary. If the man feels the need for a knife, then clearly the sex is *not* voluntary.

In the same way, people say that taxation is part of the social contract that they have voluntarily agreed to.

This is both logically and empirically false.

We know that it is empirically false because *no social contract exists*. Neither you nor I *ever* signed a document voluntarily consenting to the income tax – we were simply born into a system that takes our money from us at the point of a gun.

THE GUN IN THE ROOM

Many people will argue at this point that taxation is not enforced at the point of a gun, but rather that people pay it voluntarily. For instance, I have never had a gun pointed in my face by a tax collector or a policeman, but I have paid taxes for decades.

This may be true, but it is completely irrelevant. If I tell a woman that I will kill her children if she does not have sex with me, and she submits herself to me, we clearly understand that an immoral action has taken place – even though I have used no weapon in my violation. Clearly, if the woman submits to me, it is because she fears that I will carry out my threat. If I told her that my pet leprechaun will kill her children if she does not have sex with me, she would very likely be disturbed, but would not fear my threat in any significant way, since it is impossible for my pet leprechaun to kill her children. Or, if I died, and my will stated that I would kill this woman's children if she did not have sex with me, clearly she would feel relieved rather than afraid, since I cannot conceivably act out my threat from beyond the grave.

Thus we pay taxes because we know that if we do not, the likelihood of being aggressed against by representatives of the state is very high. If I do not pay my taxes, I will get a letter, then another letter, then a phone call, then a summons to court – and if I do not appear in court, or do not pay my back taxes and accumulated fines and interest, policemen will come with guns to take me to jail. If I resist those policemen, they will shoot me down.

To say that force equals voluntarism is completely illogical and self-contradictory. To say that the initiation of the use of force is completely equal to the non-initiation of the use of force is to say that up is down, black is white, and truth is falsehood.

Without the "null zone," these corrupt fictions cannot be sustained.

The "null zone" is the lair of the beast we hunt.

As we can see, we know that personally it is wrong to steal; we have very few problems with an abstract and logical ban on theft, such as we have worked out above – yet still, there exists this "null zone" or alternate universe where such oppositions can be accepted without any question or concern.

According to UPB, it is wrong for me and you to steal. Yet somehow, in this "null zone," it is not only allowed, but also perfectly *moral*, for others to steal. We *must not* steal – they *must* steal. It is moral madness!

POLICEMEN

Let us take our good friend Bob away from his little room of moral theory testing and restore him to his original job as a policeman.

Clearly, when Bob wakes up in the morning, before his shift, he cannot go to his neighbour's house and demand money at the point of a gun, no matter who tells him that it's all right.

When Bob has his breakfast, he also cannot attack his neighbour and take his money. On his drive to work – even though he has put on his uniform – he has not punched in yet, and thus has no more rights than any other citizen. When he punches in, however, now, as if there descends an amoral pillar of fire from the very heavens, he gains the amazing ability to morally attack his neighbours and take their money.

Strangely, this is the only characteristic of his that has utterly reversed itself. He cannot fly, he cannot change his shape, he cannot successfully digest ball bearings or live in an inferno; he cannot run 1,000 miles an hour, and neither can he walk through a brick wall. He is absolutely, utterly, and completely *the same man as he was* **before** *he punched in* – yet now, he is subject to completely opposite moral rules.

Even more strangely, if I am not a "policeman," but I follow Bob to work, and do exactly what he does – I put on a costume, walk into the police station, and put a piece of cardboard into a punch clock – why, if I then do exactly what Bob does, I am completely and totally immoral, although Bob's identical actions are completely and totally *moral*.

What kind of sense does this make? How can we conceivably unravel this impenetrable mystery?

The simple fact is that it *cannot* be unravelled, because it is completely deranged. The fact that this "opposite world" moral madness is completely irrational – not to mention violently exploitive – is so obvious that it must be buried in an endless cavalcade of mythological "voluntarism."

We are told that we "want" Bob to take our money – which completely contradicts the fact that Bob shows up on our doorstep pointing a loaded gun in our face. By this logic, I can also go up and down the street stealing money from my neighbours, and then claim to be utterly shocked when I am arrested:

"They *want* me to take their money!"

"But then why were you threatening to shoot them if they did not give you their money?"

"Because they *owe* me their money!"

"I thought you said that they want to give you their money."

"No, no – they owe me. It's really *my* money!"

"On what grounds do they owe you this money?"

"We have a contract!"

"Can you show me this contract? Have they signed this contract of their own free will?"

"It's not that kind of contract! It's a – *social* contract… And besides – according to that social contract, I own the whole street anyway – the whole damn neighbourhood in fact! Anyone who refuses to pay me my money can move somewhere else – I'm not forcing anyone!"

"And how do you know that you own the whole neighbourhood? Do you have ownership papers?"

"Yes, of course – have a look here!"

"Well, this is just a handwritten note saying that you own the whole neighbourhood – and it's the same handwriting as your signature. I'm afraid that we're going to have to book you – this is just a made-up contract with yourself, which you are inflicting on other people at the point of a gun."

This is as completely insane and corrupt as me continuing to tell a woman I am raping that she *wants* to have sex with me. Can you imagine if I were on trial for rape, and there was a videotape of the woman begging me to stop, and I had a knife to her throat, how my defense would be received if I continued to insist that she actually *wanted* to have sex with me?

In court, I would be reviled, and thrown into jail for my obvious, mad, corrupt and self-serving hypocrisy.

Ah, but in the "null zone" of government, rape is lovemaking, kidnapping is invitation, rejecting theft is evil selfishness, and coercion is kindness.

This is what I mean when I say that this "opposite world *null zone*" is the most fundamental barrier to human happiness the world over. Stealing is wrong for us; stealing is wrong in the abstract – but stealing is somehow "right" in this insane alternate universe called "government"?

PRACTICALITY

Once the violence of government is intellectually exposed – and the supposed "voluntarism" of citizens is revealed as a vicious fraud – the argument always comes back that we *need* government to supply us with public goods such as protection, regional defense, roads etc.

I have written dozens of articles exposing the falsehood of this position, so I will not bother to reiterate those arguments here, since they are not essential to a book on morality, but rather would be more appropriate to a book explaining the principles and practicalities of a voluntary society. (You can visit www.freedomainradio.com as well, where you can download hundreds of free podcasts addressing a wide variety of these topics.)

The "argument from practicality" in no way solves the problem of violence. If I see you eating cheeseburgers every day, I can tell you that it is impractical for you to do so, if you want to maintain a healthy weight. I cannot claim that it is *evil* for you to eat cheeseburgers, for reasons that we have gone into already. I cannot justly compel you through force to increase the "practicality" of your actions.

Thus saying that the government is justified in forcing us to become more "practical" is completely false, which is verified by the UPB framework – even if we assume that government solutions are more "practical," which in fact they are not.

Also, if government representatives claim that a social contract allows them to force an "impractical" population to behave more "practically," an insurmountable contradiction is created.

If I force a woman to marry a man I have chosen for her, then clearly I believe that I have infinitely better judgment about the suitability of a husband for her than she does. In fact, I do not believe that she is open to reason at all, or has any clue about her own self-interest, because I am taking *no* account of her preferences, but am forcing her to marry a man of my choosing.

When I force this woman to get married, I can only justify the use of force – even on immediate, pragmatic grounds – by claiming that she is mentally unfit to make her own choices with regards to marriage.

If the woman is mentally unfit to make her own choices with regards to marriage, then clearly she is also *mentally unfit to delegate a representative to make that choice for her.* If she has no idea what constitutes a good or suitable husband, then how can she evaluate *me* as fit to decide who will be a good or suitable husband for her?

If a man of extraordinarily low intelligence does not understand the concept of "health," would it be reasonable to expect him to be rational in his choice of a doctor? In order to competently choose a doctor, we must understand the concepts of health, efficacy, cost, professionalism and so on.

In the same way, if I do not allow a woman to have any say in who she marries, then clearly I must believe that she has no understanding of what makes a good husband – but if she has no understanding of what makes a good husband, then she has no capacity to transfer that choice to me, since she will have no way of evaluating *my* criteria for what makes a good husband.

If I cannot decide what color to paint my house, and my solution is to sign a contract with a painter allowing him to choose the color for me – and in that contract I sign away all my future freedoms to resist his decisions, and give him the right to kidnap and enslave me if I disagree with any of his decisions, or refuse to pay for them – then clearly I am not of sound mind. If I give someone the power to compel me *for the rest of my life*, then clearly I do not believe that I am competent to make my own decisions.

If I do not think that I am competent to make my own decisions, then clearly my decision to subject myself to violence *for the rest of my life* is an incompetent decision.

Either I am capable of making competent decisions, or I am not. If I *am* capable of making competent decisions, then subjecting myself to force for the rest of my life is invalid. If I am *not* capable of making competent decisions, then my decision to subject myself to force for the rest of my life is also invalid.

Even if the above considerations are somehow bypassed, however, it is still impossible to justly enforce a social contract through a government.

Clearly, I cannot sign a contract on *your* behalf, or on my children's behalf, which will be binding upon you or them for the rest of time. I cannot buy a car, send you the bill, and justly demand that you pay it. If I claim the power to impose unilateral contracts on you, UPB also grants *you* this power, and so you will just return the contract to me in my name.

In the same way, even if I choose to pay my taxes voluntarily, I cannot justly impose that choice upon you, since a voluntary contract is a merely personal preference, and so cannot be universally enforced through violence.

THE NECESSITY OF THE STATE?

This whole question becomes even more ludicrous when we look at the most common moral "justification" for the power of democratic governments, which is based upon the "will of the majority."

First of all, "will" is an aspect of the individual, while "majority" is a conceptual tag for a group. The "majority" can no more have a "will" than a "chorus line" can "give birth." If you doubt this, just try building a tree house with the concept "forest" rather than with any individual pieces of wood.

Two additional objections constantly recur whenever the question of the necessity of a government arises. The first is that a free society is only possible if people are perfectly good or rational – in other words, that citizens *need* a centralized government because there are evil people in the world.

The first and most obvious problem with this position is that if evil people exist in society, they will also exist within the government – and be far more dangerous thereby. Citizens can protect themselves against evil individuals, but stand no chance against an aggressive government armed to the teeth with police and military might. Thus the argument that we need the government because evil people exist is false. If evil people exist, the government *must* be dismantled, since evil people will be drawn to use its power for their own ends – and, unlike private thugs, evil people in government have the police and military to inflict their whims on a helpless (and relatively disarmed) population.

Thus the argument is akin to the idea that "counterfeiters are very dangerous, so we should provide an exclusive monopoly over counterfeiting to a small group of individuals." Where on earth do people think the counterfeiters will go first? (See: *Federal Reserve.*)

Logically, there are four possibilities as to the mixture of good and evil people in the world:

1. All men are moral.
2. All men are immoral.
3. The majority of men are immoral, and a minority moral.
4. The majority of men are moral, and a minority immoral.

(A perfect balance of good and evil is practically impossible.)

In the first case (*all men are moral*), the government is obviously not needed, since evil cannot exist.

In the second case (*all men are immoral*), the government cannot be permitted to exist for one simple reason. The government, it is generally argued, must exist because there are evil people in the world who desire to inflict harm, and who can only be restrained through fear of government retribution (police, prisons *et al*). A corollary of this argument is that the less retribution these people fear, the more evil they will do.

However, the government *itself* is not subject to any force or retribution, but is a law unto itself. Even in Western democracies, how many policemen and politicians go to jail?

Thus if evil people wish to do harm, but are only restrained by force, then society can *never* permit a government to exist, because evil people will work feverishly to grab control of that government, in order to do evil and avoid retribution. In a society of pure evil, then, the only hope for stability would be a state of nature, where a general arming and fear of retribution would blunt the evil intents of disparate groups. As is the case between nuclear-armed nations, a "balance of power" breeds peace.

The third possibility is that *most* people are evil, and only a few are good. If that is the case, then the government also cannot be permitted to exist, since the majority of those in control of the government will be evil, and will rule despotically over the good minority. Democracy in particular cannot be permitted, since the minority of good people would be subjugated to the democratic control of the evil majority. Evil people, who wish to do harm without fear of retribution, would inevitably control the government, and use its power to do evil free of the fear of consequences.

Good people do not act morally because they fear retribution, but because they love virtue and peace of mind – and thus, unlike evil people, they have little to gain by controlling the government. In this scenario, then, the government will inevitably be controlled by a majority of evil people who will rule over all, to the detriment of all moral people.

The fourth option is that most people are good, and only a few are evil. This possibility is subject to the same problems outlined above, notably that evil people will always want to gain control over the government, in order to shield themselves from just retaliation for their crimes. This option only changes the *appearance* of democracy: because the majority of people are good, evil power-seekers must lie to them in order to gain power, and then, after achieving public office, will immediately break faith and pursue their own corrupt agendas, enforcing their wills through the police and the military. (This is the current situation in democracies, of course.) Thus the government remains the greatest prize to the most evil men, who will quickly gain control over its awesome power – to the detriment of all good souls – and so the government cannot be permitted to exist in this scenario either.

It is clear, then, that there is no situation under which a government can logically or morally be allowed to exist. The only possible justification for the existence of a government would be if the majority of men are evil, but all the power of the government is always controlled by a minority of good men (see Plato's *Republic*).

This situation, while interesting theoretically, breaks down logically because:

a. The evil majority would quickly outvote the minority or overpower them through a coup;
b. There is no way to ensure that only good people would always run the government; and,
c. There is absolutely no example of this having ever occurred in any of the brutal annals of state history.

The logical error always made in the defense of the government is to imagine that any collective moral judgments being applied to any group of people *is not also being applied to the group which rules over them.* If 50% of people are evil, then *at least* 50% of people ruling over them are also evil (and probably more, since evil people are always drawn to power). Thus the existence of evil can never justify the existence of a government.

If there is no evil, governments are unnecessary. If evil exists, the governments are far too dangerous to be allowed to exist.

Why is this error so prevalent?

There are a number of reasons, which can only be touched on here. The first is that the government introduces itself to children in the form of public school teachers who are considered moral authorities. Thus are *morality* and *authority* first associated with the government – an association that is then reinforced through years of grinding repetition.

The second is that the government never teaches children about the root of its power – violence – but instead pretends that it is just another social institution, like a business or a church or a charity, but more moral.

The third is that the prevalence of religion and propaganda has always blinded men to the evils of the government – which is why rulers have always been so interested in furthering the interests of churches and state "education." In the religious world-view, absolute power is synonymous with perfect virtue, in the form of a deity. In the real political world of men, however, increasing power always means increasing evil. With religion, also, all that happens must be for the good – thus, fighting encroaching political power is fighting the will of the deity. There are many more reasons, of course, but these are among the deepest. (For a more detailed discussion of the role that *parents* play in inculcating the fantasy that "power equals virtue," please see my book "On Truth: The Tyranny of Illusion.")

At the beginning of this section, I mentioned that people generally make *two* errors when confronted with the idea of dissolving the government. The first is the belief that governments are necessary because evil people exist. The second is the belief that, in the absence of governments, any social institutions that arise will inevitably take the place of governments. Thus, Dispute Resolution Organizations (DROs), insurance companies and private security forces are all considered potential cancers that will swell and overwhelm the body politic.

This view arises from the same error outlined above. If *all* social institutions are constantly trying to grow in power and enforce their wills on others, then by that very argument a centralized government cannot be allowed to exist. If it is an iron law that groups always try to gain power over other groups and individuals, then that power-lust *will not end if one of them wins, but will continue to spread across society virtually unopposed until slavery is the norm.*

The only way that social institutions can grow into violent monopolies is *to offload the costs of enforcement onto their victims.* Governments grow endlessly because they can pay tax collectors with a portion of the taxes they collect. The slaves are thus forced to pay for the costs of their enslavement.

In a voluntary society, there would be no taxation, and thus any group wishing to gain monopolistic power would have to fund its army itself, which would never be economically feasible or profitable. (For more details, please see my article "War, Profit and the State" at www.freedomain.blogspot.com.)

It is very hard to understand the logic and intelligence of the argument that, in order to protect us from a group that *might* overpower us, we should support a group that *already has* overpowered us. It is similar to the statist argument about private monopolies – that citizens should create a governmental monopoly because they are afraid of private monopolies. It does not take keen vision to see through such nonsense.

What is the evidence for the view that decentralized and competing powers promotes peace? In other words, are there any facts that we can draw on to support the idea that a balance of power is the only chance that the individual has for freedom?

Organized crime does not provide many good examples, since gangs so regularly corrupt, manipulate and use the power of the government police to enforce their rule, and so such gangs cannot be said to be operating in a state of nature. Also, criminal gangs profit enormously by supplying legally-banned substances or services, and so also flourish largely due to state policies.

A more useful example is the fact that no leader has ever declared war on another leader who possesses nuclear weapons. In the past, when leaders felt themselves immune from personal retaliation, they were more than willing to kill off their own populations by waging war. Now that they are themselves subject to annihilation, they are only willing to attack countries that cannot fight back.

This is an instructive lesson on why such men require disarmed and dependent populations – and a good example of how the fear of reprisal inherent in a balanced system of decentralized and competing powers *is the only proven method of securing and maintaining personal liberty.*

Fleeing from imaginary devils into the protective prisons of governments only ensures the destruction of the very liberties that make life worth living.

GOVERNMENTS AND RELIGION

The idea that being born creates a contract with a fictional agency, which in practical terms makes you a quasi-slave to specific individuals, is common to both religion and the state – and one other, far more personal agency, which I talk about in my first book "On Truth: The Tyranny Of Illusion."

Whenever a priest says: "Obey God," what he is really saying is: "Obey *me*." Since God does not exist, any commandment that the priest claims is coming from God, is actually coming from the priest. "God" is just the fictional entity used to bully you conceptually in order to obtain your very practical subservience in the real world, to real individuals, in terms of voluntarily handing over money, time and resources.

It is far more efficient for exploiters to have their slaves consider slavery a virtue, since it cuts down enormously on the costs of controlling them. If I can convince you that it is evil to avoid serving me, and virtuous to be my slave, then I do not need to hire nearly as many thugs to bully, control and steal from you.

Religious and state mythologies, then, are fictions that vastly reduce the costs of controlling populations; they are the lubricant and fuel for the ghastly machinery of institutionalized violence.

Throughout the world, rulers are a very small percentage of the population. How can it be possible for 1-2% of people to control everybody else? There is a certain monopoly on armaments, to be sure, but that monopoly is relatively easy to counter, since most governments make a fortune selling weapons throughout the world.

The sad reality is that people as a whole are enslaved to fictional entities such as nations, gods, cultures – and governments.

Our personal pride would instinctively rebel against a immediate and enforced slavery to another human being – however, we seem to almost revel in slavery to *mythology.*

Our desire to be good – combined with the thrill of virtue that we get by obeying moral mythologies – has us lining up to willingly hand our resources over to those who claim to represent these mythologies.

One central reason that we know that governments and gods are unnecessary is that they are so effective. *We know that most people desperately want to be good because they are so easily controlled by moral theories.*

The logic of obedience to mythology is patently foolish. If a priest tells me that I have to obey "God," this is exactly the same as him telling me that I must obey an entity called "Nog." Even if I accept that this fictional entity is worthy of eternal obedience, this still in no way would compel me to obey *the priest*. If I tell you to "obey your heart," can I then reasonably say: "and *I alone* speak for your heart"?

Of course not.

When we strip away mythology and fiction from our "interactions" with our rulers, what emerges is a grim, stark and murderously exploitive reality.

Let's take as an example a very real and present danger: taxation.

TAXATION

I am told that, by virtue of choosing to live in Canada, I owe "the government" more than 50% of my income.

Stripped of mythology, what does this really translate to?

In reality, I will wait until the end of time for "the government" to come and pick up its money. Waiting for "the government" to drop by is like wanting to date the concept "femininity." I may as well try to pay for my dinner with the word "money."

In reality, when I am told that I must pay my taxes to "the government," what this actually means is that I must write a check to transfer my money into a particular bank account, which is then accessed by particular individuals. These individuals then have the right to take that money, and spend it as they see fit – these particular individuals thus have complete control over my money.

At no point whatsoever does any such entity as "the government" lift a finger, make a move, open a bank account, or spend a penny. Imagining that a concept called "the government" has the capacity to take or spend your money is exactly the same as waiting for "God" to come and pick you up and take you to church.

Thus the real interaction is that one guy sends me a letter telling me that I owe him money. I have no contract with this guy, and he does not in fact own any of my property, although some other guys wrote a supposed "contract" which claims that he does.

If I do not pay this guy, he will send another guy over to my house to collect the money – plus "interest" and "charges."

Normally, when a man with a gun comes to my house and demands my money, I have the right to use force to defend myself. In this case, however, because he is in a costume and claims to represent a fictional entity, I am not allowed to use force to defend myself.

Now, if I come to your house tonight dressed as a "high elf of Narnia" and demand the money that you owe to the "Queen of Sorrows," assuming it is not Halloween, you are allowed to stare at me in amazement, and order me off your property.

If I do not pay the man who comes to take my money, he is allowed to pull out a gun, point it at my chest, and kidnap me – or shoot me if I resist. He can hold me in a tiny cell for year after year, where I will be subjected to the most violent brutality and continual rape, until he chooses to let me go.

Interestingly, if a man legitimately owes me money, I am not allowed to kidnap him and subject him to torture and rape for year after year.

Thus taxation utterly violates the UPB framework, since it is the violent transfer of property using the initiation of force.

Stealing, as we have proven, is evil.

Einstein revolutionized physics by claiming – and proving – that the speed of light was constant.

We can revolutionize the world by accepting the claim – and the proof – that stealing is always evil.

Government, Religion and UPB

When we take the UPB framework and apply it to moral propositions regarding government and religion, some very interesting results occur.

The proposition that is most often used to justify government power is: "the government has the right to take your money." This, however, is an utterly imprecise and false statement. The "government" does not have the right to take your money, since "the government" is merely a concept, an abstract description for a self-defined group of people. UPB requires a more consistent and objective statement. Since moral rules must be the same for everyone in all places and at all times, we must rephrase the rule in this way:

"Human beings can morally take money from other human beings if they make up a conceptual agency that justifies their actions."

If we return to Bob and Doug in our little room of moral experimentation, we can very quickly see that this becomes an impossible proposition.

If Bob says to Doug: "I now represent the ideal concept 'FUBAR,' which fully justifies me taking your lighter from you. Since you now owe me your lighter, you must hand it over, or I will be compelled to take it from you by force."

What will Doug's reaction be? Remember, according to UPB, whatever is valid for Bob must also be valid for Doug. Inevitably, Doug will reply: "Oh yeah? Well *I* now represent the ideal concept 'ANTI-FUBAR,' which fully justifies me retaining possession of my lighter. Since you now have no right to take my lighter, if you try to take it, I will be compelled to defend myself by force."

As you can see, if *Bob* has the right to make up imaginary obligations and impose them on Doug, then *Doug* has the right to make up imaginary obligations and impose them on Bob. Clearly, we immediately end up in a perfect stalemate. If it is morally good to impose made-up obligations on other people, but it is impossible to do it if *everyone* possesses that ability, then morality becomes impossible. The only way that Bob can impose his made-up obligation on Doug is if Doug refuses to impose his made up obligation on Bob – thus we have a situation where what is moral for one person can only be achieved by the other person acting in an anti-moral manner. Virtue can thus only be enabled by vice, which is impossible – and we have opposing moral rules for two human beings in the same circumstance, which UPB instantly rejects as invalid.

In other words, every imaginary abstract justification for the use of force can be countered by another imaginary abstract justification for the use of force. If I have an imaginary friend that can justify everything I do, then *you* also can have an imaginary friend that can justify everything you do. Thus neither of us can possess the ability to impose our imaginary obligations on others.

RELIGION AND UPB
The same holds true for religion.

The statement: "You must obey me because God commands it," must be restated more accurately as: "an entity that I have made up commands you to obey me." The principle that UPB requires, then, is: "Human beings must impose unchosen positive obligations on others, and justify those obligations according to imaginary entities."

Here we see the same issues as above. Bob tells Doug: "You must give me your lighter, because my imaginary friend tells you to." Naturally, Doug replies: "You must not ask me for your lighter, because *my* imaginary friend forbids you to." If Bob's "commandments" are valid, then Doug's "commandments" are equally valid, and so cancel each other out.

In the same way, if a man claims that his concept called "the government" justifies his theft of my property, then I can claim that my concept called "the anti-government" justifies my *retention* of my property, and we are both equally "valid" in our justifications.

If this tax collector then claims that his concept called "the government" only justifies his theft of *my* property, not my retention of it, then we are no further ahead. He can take my thousand dollars, but then I can invoke my concept to "steal" that money back, and his moral theory commands us to spend the rest of eternity handing back and forth the thousand dollars.

UPB and "The Majority"
UPB does not allow for the accumulation of individuals to override or reverse the properties of each individual. Ten lions do not make an elephant, a government, or a god. Ten thousand soldiers might make an "army," but they cannot reverse gravity, or make murder moral.

Returning one last time to the room of Bob and Doug, let's introduce "Jane."

Now that there are three people in the room, we can look at the "majority rule" principle.

If Bob, Doug and Jane take a "vote" on whether or not it is moral to rape Jane, we would all recoil at such an unjust and immoral premise. Clearly, even if Jane were "outvoted," we would not consider the resulting rape to be transformed into a morally good act.

Why not?

Well, UPB does not recognize the reality of aggregations, since the "majority" is a mere conceptual tag; it does not exist in reality, any more than "gods" or "governments" do. Thus to claim that the concept of "the majority" has any sort of moral standing is utterly invalid – it is like saying that "the Fatherland" can impregnate a woman, or that one can sit in the word "chair."

To say that "the majority" has rights or attributes which directly contradict the rights or attributes of any individual also contradicts rational principles, since any conceptual grouping is only validated by the accurate identification of individual characteristics. If I say that "mammals" are warm-blooded living creatures, can I logically include three plastic flamingos in the category "mammal"?

Of course not.

Thus if it is evil for human beings to rape, can I logically create a category called "the majority" and then claim that for *these* human beings, rape is now morally good?

Of *course* not.

MAJORITY RULE

Can I create a moral rule that says: "the majority should be able to do whatever it wants"?

Of course I can, but it will never be valid or true.

Only *individuals* act – the "majority" never does. If moral rules can change when a certain number of people get together, then UPB is continually violated.

If it is moral for Bob and Doug to rape Jane because they have "outvoted her," what happens when Jane's two friends show up and vote against Bob and Doug's infernal desires?

Well, suddenly Bob and Doug are the ones outvoted, and rape becomes "evil" for them again.

Nothing substantial has changed in these "outvoting" scenarios, but we have a series of opposing moral rules for the same men – a violation of UPB, and thus invalid.

Rape cannot be good, then evil, then good again, just because a few hands are raised or lowered.

Thus if you think that "majority rule" sounds like a reasonable moral proposition, and a perfectly valid moral theory, then I am afraid you're going to have to go back to the beginning of this book and start again! ☺

Additional Proofs

• • •

There are other additional proofs that we can bring to bear on the question of universally preferable behaviour.

The free-market economy

A free-market economy is without a doubt the most efficient and wealth-producing method of organizing the production and consumption of goods and resources within society. Its material success is without equal in human history, or across the world.

The framework of UPB anticipates, validates and explains the reasons for the material successes of a free market economy.

In theory, a free-market economy is based on the application of a universal theory of property rights. By contrast, communism is based on the explicit rejection of a universal theory of property rights. Since we have proven above that universal property rights is the only valid moral theory, this explains at the most fundamental level why communism is such a disaster, while a free-market economy is so materially productive.

Since human beings *do in fact* have equal rights of property, any social system which rejects this right is doomed to utter failure – just as any bridge planner who rejects the reality of gravity will never be able to build a bridge that stands.

THE SCIENTIFIC METHOD

Logic and science are in fact methodologies which exist – along with morality – under the umbrella of UPB. In other words, logic and science are both validated by the framework of UPB.

A central question which needs to be answered is: *why is the scientific method infinitely superior to other "methodologies" of knowledge acquisition, such as mysticism?*

UPB answers this question.

Since any methodology for knowledge acquisition must be universal, consistent, and independent of time and place, the scientific method meets these requirements, while irrational and subjective mysticism is the exact opposite of these requirements.

PUBLIC EDUCATION

One central principle of free market economics is that quality only really results from *voluntarism*. Coercion, fundamentally, is inefficient – violence always results in poor quality. The old-style Soviet bakeries never carried good bread; a man who beats his wife will never have a happy marriage.

The initiation of the use of force is always counter to any rational moral theory – it is a specific and explicit violation of UPB. Since public schools are funded through the initiation of the use of force, they are a form of *forced association*, which is a clear violation of the *freedom of association* validated by UPB.

Since force violates the moral requirement of *avoidability* – and a lack of avoidability always breeds poor quality – UPB would help us easily predict that public schools would provide education of low quality.

Furthermore, UPB would also have helped us predict that, as more and more force was used in the realm of public education – as taxes, union compulsions and so on escalated – the quality of the education provided would get worse and worse.

This, of course, was – and is – exactly the case.

PARALLELS

• • •

BEFORE THE SCIENTIFIC REVOLUTION, IT was considered inconceivable that the natural world could sustain itself without a conscious and "moral" entity at its centre. The sun rose trailing the chains of a supernatural chariot; the moon was a cold and lonely brother of the sun. Constellations outlined the tales and graves of the gods, and storms stemmed from the rage of demons.

The idea that nature was a self-generating and self-sustaining system was almost unimaginable. The Darwinian revolution, the idea that life was not created, but rather evolved, brought this idea from the material to the biological world.

Before science, at the centre of every complex system lay a virtuous consciousness – without which this system would fly into chaos, and cease to be.

Unfortunately, this "virtuous consciousness" was merely an illusion, to put it most charitably. No such gods existed – all that *did* exist were the pronouncements of priests. Thus what really lay at the centre was the bias of irrational individuals, who had no idea how mad they really were.

We have yet to apply this same illumination to our conceptions of society – but it is now *essential* that we do so.

We consider it essential that, at the centre of society, we place a virtuous entity called "the government." In the absence of this entity, we consider it axiomatic that society will fly into chaos, and cease to be – just as our ancestors considered that, in the absence of gods, the universe itself would fly into chaos, and cease to be.

However, "the government" no more exists than "god" exists.

When we speak of "gods," we are really talking about "the opinions of priests."

When we speak of "the government," we *really* mean "the violence of a tiny minority."

The idea of "spontaneous order," which is well proven in the realms of physics and biology, remains largely inconceivable to us in the realm of society.

However, "governments" are no more needed for the organization and continuance of society than "gods" are required for the organization and continuance of the universe.

In fact, just as religions impeded the progress of science, so do governments impede the progress of society. Just as the illusions of *religion* caused the deaths of hundreds of millions of people throughout history, so have the illusions of *government*.

Just as the false ethics of religions "justify" all manners of abuse, corruption and violence, so do the false ethics of governments.

When we choose to live by fantasy, we inevitably choose destruction, in one form or another.

When we choose to run society according to religious moral mythologies, we end up with wars, violence, repression, abuse, corruption and bottomless hypocrisy.

When we choose to run society according to *statist* moral mythologies, the results are no different.

We can either choose virtue or compulsion.

We cannot have both.

SOLUTIONS

We can choose to believe that the government is both a necessary and a moral institution. We can choose to believe that, without government, society will collapse into "anarchy," and the world will dissolve into a war of all against all. We can choose to believe that without the government, there will be no roads, no education, no healthcare, no old-age pensions, no libraries, no protection of property and so on.

Similar superstitions, of course, have retarded the progress of mankind throughout history. The most significant precursor to what UPB reveals about the government is what science revealed about religion.

As science began to practically postulate a universe that could run without a god, all manner of hysterics clamoured that the end of the world was nigh, that society would collapse into "anarchy," and that civilization would dissolve into a war of all against all.

Any time a system that justifies power can be conceived of running *without* that power, all those who profit from the manipulation of that power cry out that without them, all is lost.

Priests did this during the onset of the scientific revolution. Without God, life has no meaning. Without God, man has no morality. Without God, our souls cannot be saved. Without God, the world will descend into chaos and evil.

None of it turned out to be true, of course. In fact, quite the *reverse* turned out to be true. The end of religion as the dominant world-view paved the way for the separation of church and state, the end of the aristocracy, the rise of the free market, the establishment of many human liberties in significant areas of the world.

The fall of God was the rise of mankind.

In the same way, when we begin see society as the early scientists saw the universe – as a self-sustaining system without the need for an imaginary central authority – then we can truly begin to perceive the possibilities of freedom for mankind.

The establishment of a central and coercive monopoly in society perpetually retards the progress of knowledge, of wisdom, of virtue, of physical and mental health – just as the establishment of a central and coercive monopoly in the *universe* perpetually retarded the progress of knowledge, of wisdom, and science.

The way to oppose imaginary entities is with relentless truth. The way to oppose God is with reason, evidence and science.

The way to oppose the state – the most dangerous imaginary entity – is with reason, evidence and science.

The Future

Whether we like it or not, UPB applies to everything that we do. Human beings have a natural tendency towards consistency, since we are beings with a rational consciousness, inhabiting a consistent and rational universe. Thus whatever premises we accept in our lives tend to compel more and more consistent behaviour throughout our lives – and throughout the "life" of our culture or nation as well.

Thus a man who believes that bullying is a good way to get what he wants tends to bully more and more over the course of his lifetime. A man who believes that violence is good tends to become more and more violent.

In other words, UPB demands consistency even in inconsistency. UPB demands uniformity even in immorality

The root moral premises of a culture thus dictate its inevitable future. A culture built on justifications for coercion will always become more coercive. A culture built on rational liberty will always become less coercive.

That is why the delineation of a rational framework for ethics is so essential.

What we believe is what we become.

If we believe lies, we shall become slaves.

CONCLUSIONS

• • •

IN A RELATIVELY SHORT TIME, we have covered an enormous amount of ground. The greatest challenge of philosophy is the definition of a universal, objective and absolute morality that does not rely on God or the state. The moment that we rely on God or the state for the definition of morality, morality no longer remains universal, objective and absolute. In other words, it is no longer "morality."

The invention of imaginary entities such as "God" and "the state" does *nothing* to answer our questions about morality.

We fully understand that the invention of God did nothing – and does nothing – to answer questions about the origin of life, or the universe. To say, in answer to any question, "some incomprehensible being did some inconceivable thing in some unfathomable manner for unknowable purposes," cannot be considered any sort of rational answer.

The gravest danger in making up incomprehensible "answers" to rational and essential questions is that it provides the *illusion* of an answer, which in general negates the pursuit of truth. Furthermore, a group inevitably coalesces to defend and profit from this irrational non-answer.

In the realm of religion, this is the priestly caste. In the realm of government, this is the political caste.

When a real and essential question is met with a mystical and violent "answer," human progress turns to regression. The science of meteorology fails to come into being if the priests say that the rain comes because the gods will it. The science of medicine fails to develop if illness is considered a moral punishment from the gods. The science of physics stalls and regresses if the motion of the stars is considered the clockwork of the deities.

When false answers are presented to moral questions, questioning those answers inevitably becomes a moral crime. When illusions are substituted for curiosity, those who profit from those illusions inevitably end up using violence to defend their lies.

And for evermore, *children* are the first victims of these exploitive falsehoods.

Children do not have to be bullied into eating candy, playing tag, or understanding that two plus two is four. The human mind does not require that the truth be inflicted through terror, boredom, insults and repetition. A child does not have to be "taught" that a toy is real by telling him that he is damned to hell for eternity if he does not *believe* that the toy is real. A child does not have to be bullied into believing that chocolate tastes good by being told that his taste buds are damned by original sin.

Saying that morality exists because God tells us that it exists is exactly the same as saying that morality does not exist. If you buy an iPod from me on eBay, and I send you an empty box, you will write to me in outrage. If I tell you not to worry, that my invisible friend assures me that there is in fact an iPod in the box, would you be satisfied? Would not my claim that my invisible friend tells me of the iPod's existence be a certain proof that the iPod did not in fact exist?

If morality is justified according to the authority of a being that does not exist, then morality by definition is not justified. If I write a check that is "certified" by a bank that does not exist, then clearly my check is by definition *invalid*.

The same is true for enforcing morality through the irrational monopoly of "the state." If we allow the existence of a government – a minority of people who claim the right to initiate the use of force, a right which is specifically denied to everyone else – then any and all moral "rules" enforced by the government are purely subjective, since the government is *by definition* based on a violation of moral rules.

If I say that I need the government to protect my property, but that the government is by definition a group of people who can violate my property rights at will, then I am caught in an insurmountable contradiction. I am saying that my property rights must be defended – and then I create an agency to defend them that can violate them at any time. This is like being so afraid of rape that I hire a bodyguard to protect me from being raped – but in the contract, I allow my bodyguard – and anyone he chooses – to rape me at will.

Because "morality" based on the state and on religion is so irrational and self-contradictory, it *requires* a social agency with a monopoly on the initiation of force to function. Since everyone is just making up "morals" and claiming absolute justification based on imaginary entities, rational negotiation and understanding remain impossible. We do not need a government because people are bad, but rather, because people are irrational, we end up with a government. False moral theories always end up requiring violence to enforce them. Moral theories are not developed in *response* to violence – false moral theories *cause* violence – in fact, *demand* violence.

The moral subjectivism and irrationality involved in answering "What is truth?" with "God," and "What is morality?" with "government," is so openly revealed by the framework of UPB that it is hard to imagine that this concept is not more widespread.

One central reason for this is that truly understanding UPB requires the very highest possible mental functioning. It is relatively easy to be rational; it is very difficult to think about the implicit premises of rationality, and all that they entail. It is relatively easy to debate; it is very difficult to tease out all of the implicit assumptions involved in the very act of debating.

It is easy to catch a ball – it is hard to invent the physics that explain motion *universally.*

Thinking *about* thinking is the hardest mental discipline of all.

At the beginning of this book, I talked about a "beast" that terrified and enslaved mankind. This beast is always located on a mountaintop, or in a deep cave. People are afraid of the beast in the world, which is why the beast has never been defeated.

The beast has never been defeated because the beast is an illusion.

The beast cannot be defeated in the world, because the beast is within ourselves.

The collective fantasy that there exists a "null zone," where morality magically reverses itself, called "the government" is exactly the same as the collective fantasy that there exists a "null zone" called "God" where *reality* reverses itself.

If we define "morality" according to the subjective fantasies of mere mortals, then it will forever remain under the manipulative control of power-hungry tyrants. Since God does not exist, anyone who speaks about morality in relation to God is just making up definitions to serve his own purposes.

Since "the state" does not exist, anyone who speaks about morality in relation to government is just making up definitions to serve his own purposes.

Until we can define an objective and rational morality that is free from the subjective whims of each individual, we will never make the kind of progress that we need to as a species.

Morality, like physics, biology, geology and chemistry, must join the realm of the sciences if we are to flourish – and indeed, perhaps, to survive at all.

However, if we can sustain our courage, it is this discipline alone that can set us, and our children – and all humanity in the future – free from the tyranny of the greatest beast: our own moral illusions.

• • •

BELOW, PLEASE FIND A SUMMATION of the core argument for morality.

1. Reality is objective and consistent.
2. "Logic" is the set of objective and consistent rules derived from the consistency of reality.
3. Those theories that conform to logic are called "valid."
4. Those theories that are confirmed by empirical testing are called "accurate."
5. Those theories that are both valid and accurate are called "true."
6. "Preferences" are required for life, thought, language and debating.
7. Debating requires that both parties hold "truth" to be both objective and universally preferable.
8. Thus the very act of debating contains an acceptance of universally preferable behaviour (UPB).
9. Theories regarding UPB must pass the tests of logical consistency and empirical verification.
10. The subset of UPB that examines enforceable behaviour is called "morality."
11. As a subset of UPB, no moral theory can be considered true if it is illogical or unsupported by empirical evidence.
12. Moral theories that are supported by logic and evidence are true. All other moral theories are false.

• • •

BELOW IS A SAMPLE TABLE that lists some of the most common categories of actions/ rules, and their key differentiators.

Action / Rule	Preference?	Universal?	Enforceable?	Requires initiating action on the part of the victim?	Can violators be avoided?	Moral Category
Running for the bus.	No	No	n/a	n/a	n/a	Neutral
You should not like ice cream.	Yes	No	No	n/a	n/a	Neutral (personal preference)
You should not be late.	Yes	Yes	No	No	Yes	APA
You should not commit fraud.	Yes	Yes	Yes	Yes	Yes	Good
You should not rape.	Yes	Yes	Yes	No	No	Good

• • •

UPB Sceptic: UPB is invalid.

Me: How do you know?

UPB Sceptic: It's not proven!

Me: So "proof" is UPB?

UPB Sceptic: No, nothing is UPB.

Me: Isn't the statement "nothing is UPB" UPB?

UPB Sceptic: No, that's not what I'm saying at all! I'm saying that UPB is invalid!

Me: Why?

UPB Sceptic: Because it's false!

Me: So presenting true arguments is UPB?

UPB Sceptic: No!

Me: So there's nothing wrong with false arguments?

UPB Sceptic: No.

Me: Then why are you opposing a false argument?

UPB Sceptic: Oh, it's just my personal preference. I just dislike falsehood.

Me: So you're arguing for a merely personal preference?

UPB Sceptic: Sure!

Me: So why should your personal preference take precedence over mine? I like UPB, you don't – and why bother debating personal preferences at all?

UPB Sceptic: Oh - because UPB is invalid!

Me: Why is it invalid?

UPB Sceptic: Because it's self-contradictory!

Me: So consistency is UPB?

UPB Sceptic: No! And stop repeating the same points over and over! And go read Kant / Hegel / Hume etc.

INDEX

Illusion(s), 8, 21, 22, 26, 141, 174, 178, 181

illusions. *See* "Illusion(s)"

Jazz, 30, 40, 57, 99, 100

Knowledge, 13, 18, 20, 25, 30, 53, 54, 72, 82, 89, 119, 140, 173, 176, 177

Language, 11, 32, 33, 43, 46, 48, 50, 52, 183

Law, 13, 54, 78, 148, 159, 162

Lies, 9, 18, 19, 82, 84, 87, 177, 179

Logic, 34, 35, 68, 172, 183

Logical, 8, 15, 19, 20, 39, 44, 49, 54, 55, 56, 57, 62, 64, 65, 67, 68, 94, 95, 96, 98, 99, 100, 101, 103, 104, 107, 108, 116, 119, 129, 134, 135, 136, 140, 142, 144, 152, 160, 183

Mathematics, 42, 44, 140, 143

Monopoly, 9, 158, 162, 164, 176, 177, 179, 180

Moral Rule, 18, 54, 77, 93, 94, 97, 98, 100, 134, 149, 170

Moral Rules, 9, 11, 53, 54, 55, 56, 57, 58, 59, 61, 65, 66, 85, 98, 100, 108, 120, 139, 146, 147, 148, 149, 150, 152, 167, 168, 170, 171, 179

Morality, 8, 9, 10, 11, 12, 13, 15, 20, 21, 54, 55, 59, 61, 62, 68, 71, 82, 83, 84, 86, 93, 96, 98, 102, 108, 110, 112, 114, 115, 117, 135, 136, 140, 147, 149, 155, 161, 168, 172, 176, 178, 179, 180, 181, 183, 185

Murder, 13, 14, 18, 19, 21, 39, 40, 54, 58, 63, 64, 65, 67, 68, 71, 72, 78, 85, 92, 93, 94,

106, 107, 108, 109, 112, 113, 114, 122, 123, 126, 127, 131, 132, 139, 140, 145, 146, 148, 149, 150, 169, 186

Mythology, 10, 164, 165

Opinion, 15, 31, 48, 49, 50, 78, 149

Parents, 8, 60, 88, 129, 131, 132, 161

Physical Laws, 17, 37, 55, 58

Physics, 18, 25, 31, 32, 34, 39, 40, 42, 54, 55, 56, 60, 62, 64, 65, 66, 76, 78, 92, 139, 140, 143, 146, 166, 175, 178, 180, 181

Plato, 9, 12, 160

Politicians, 8, 55, 81, 159

Priests, 8, 21, 55, 81, 86, 87, 174, 178

Proof, 11, 15, 30, 42, 58, 105, 141, 166, 179, 187

Property Rights, 26, 64, 65, 66, 80, 83, 94, 110, 112, 113, 116, 117, 118, 119, 120, 136, 172, 180

Rand, Ayn, 9, 83

Rape, 13, 18, 39, 40, 58, 61, 65, 67, 72, 74, 85, 92, 94, 95, 96, 97, 98, 99, 100, 101, 102, 103, 104, 105, 106, 107, 108, 109, 113, 122, 123, 126, 127, 128, 130, 133, 134, 139, 150, 154, 166, 169, 170, 180, 184

Rationality, 26, 31, 35, 36, 53, 65, 69, 143, 144, 180

Reality, 11, 12, 14, 17, 21, 24, 26, 32, 33, 34, 35, 36, 38, 41, 42, 44, 45, 52, 54, 55, 59, 61, 64, 86, 114, 117, 125, 142, 144, 145, 149, 150, 164, 165, 169, 172, 181, 183, 185

Reason, 10, 11, 12, 14, 30, 38, 50, 69, 72, 76,
81, 87, 94, 101, 104, 112, 130, 131, 134,
142, 143, 145, 147, 155, 158, 164,
177, 180
Relativism, 81
Religion, 19, 21, 26, 140, 161, 163, 167, 168,
175, 176, 178, 180

Scientific Method, 9, 11, 13, 26, 31, 34, 42,
44, 47, 53, 54, 55, 59, 61, 65, 67, 68, 82, 94,
173, 185
Society, 12, 25, 63, 145, 146, 147, 155, 157,
158, 159, 162, 172, 174, 175, 176
Socrates, 9, 20
Soldiers, 63, 146, 148, 169
Subjective, 9, 12, 17, 19, 31, 32, 42, 46, 48, 49,
53, 55, 57, 60, 61, 62, 81, 94, 99, 126, 129,
130, 141, 147, 173, 179, 181
Subjectivism, 12, 13, 41, 53, 83, 115, 180

Superstition, 8, 21, 22, 27

Taxation, 10, 88, 147, 150, 151, 162, 165, 166
Theft, 13, 18, 65, 67, 80, 85, 93, 94, 108, 109,
110, 114, 117, 118, 119, 121, 122, 123, 126,
127, 134, 139, 147, 152, 154, 168, 169

Universally Preferable Behaviour, 53, 56, 57,
58, 59, 60, 61, 92, 96, 100, 102, 104, 110,
172, 183
UPB. *See* "Universally Preferable
Behaviour"

Violence, 9, 10, 18, 21, 50, 65, 68, 69, 71, 73,
81, 84, 89, 92, 98, 100, 102, 124, 125, 126,
127, 128, 154, 155, 156, 157, 161, 164, 173,
175, 177, 179, 180
Virtue, 8, 9, 19, 63, 86, 87, 88, 93, 94, 95, 98,
106, 127, 149, 159, 161, 164, 165, 175, 176

Made in the USA
Middletown, DE
25 October 2018